Adolf E. Hieke / Elsa Lattey   Using Idioms

Adolf E. Hieke / Elsa Lattey

Using Idioms: Situationsbezogene Redensarten

Max Niemeyer Verlag
Tübingen 1983

CIP-Kurztitelaufnahme der Deutschen Bibliothek

Hieke, Adolf E.:
Using idioms: situationsbezogene Redensarten / Adolf E. Hieke ; Elsa Lattey.
- Tübingen : Niemeyer, 1983
NE: Lattey, Elsa:

ISBN 3-484-40095-1

© Max Niemeyer Verlag Tübingen 1983
Alle Rechte vorbehalten. Ohne Genehmigung des Verlages ist es nicht gestattet, dieses Buch oder Teile daraus photomechanisch zu vervielfältigen.
Printed in Germany. Druck: Weihert-Druck GmbH, Darmstadt.

TABLE OF CONTENTS

Introduction	VII
Instructions	IX
Abbreviation Key	XI
Explanation of Terms in Idiom Entries	XI

Unit 1 *Test Yourself* — 1
    Idiom Entries and Usage
        Focus on the Individual (non-negative) — 4
    Exercises — 7

Unit 2 *Test Yourself* — 15
    Idiom Entries and Usage
        Focus on the Individual (negative) — 17
    Exercises — 19

Unit 3 *Test Yourself* — 26
    Idiom Entries and Usage
        Interaction of Individuals (positive) — 27
    Exercises — 28

Unit 4 *Test Yourself* — 33
    Idiom Entries and Usage
        Interaction of Individuals (neutral) — 35
    Exercises — 38

Unit 5 *Test Yourself* — 45
    Idiom Entries and Usage
        Interaction of Individuals (negative) — 47
    Exercises — 49

Unit 6 *Test Yourself* — 56
    Idiom Entries and Usage
        Individual and World (positive) — 58
    Exercises — 61

Unit 7 *Test Yourself* — 69
    Idiom Entries and Usage
        Individual and World (neutral) — 71
    Exercises — 73

Unit 8	*Test Yourself*	80
	Idiom Entries and Usage Individual and World (negative)	82
	Exercises	84
Unit 9	*Test Yourself*	90
	Idiom Entries and Usage Focus on the World	92
	Exercises	94
Final Check		101
Answer Key	– *Exercises*	125
	– *Final Check*	132
English Index		135
German Index		138

INTRODUCTION

The apt and timely use of an idiom is certainly one of the great variety of devices which help lubricate our discourse and bring us closer to the people we are speaking to, and not only because they may lend a native tinge to our conversation in another language.

> Idioms are therefore not only lexemes which capture complex everyday situations semantically, but they are linguistic units that reduce the complexity of social interactions. Idioms contain information on the one hand, but they also provide a method of handling special situations.*

This immediacy to communicative goals on the one hand and to rapport with one's interlocutors on the other is not easily achieved in a foreign language. Idiomatic expressions are semantically and formally complex and, when we try to assimilate them into our active vocabulary, they often prove challenging, perhaps because native speakers, if one observes them closely, tend to use idioms in a quite vague manner themselves. Even dictionaries can be surprisingly inaccurate in defining them. In going from one language to another, it proves difficult to capture the meaning and use of an idiom and to render it in idiomatic form in the foreign language. This is true particularly for opaque idioms, those whose meaning is not at all clear from the words used to express it. Consequently, it takes more than a casual perusal of idioms to grasp, incorporate and apply them in terms of one's discourse demands within the contextual constellations of another language. We have tried to let such factors guide us in our choice and treatment of idioms and to expose learners of English to our inventory of common idioms in concentrated, repeated and varied fashion.

The idioms in this workbook were chosen on the basis of high frequency in German** as well as English - as far as this can be determined - and are of the kind that resist easy translation; they are so opaque, in other words, that a German speaker of English could not be expected to render a native idiom in any way approximating its English counterpart. Conversely, following each unit we listed some idioms where the languages unexpectedly do share the same image, also a source of possible confusion to learners. We have limited our inventory to the classic variety of tournure idioms, thus excluding those having fewer than three lexemes (such as verb-adverb composites, i.e. hang on, rip off). For tighter cohesion along the lines of semantic affinity, our unit grouping follows pragmatic notions wherever possible - for instance, an individual interacting with others, an individual shown vis-à-vis the world, or primary focus on the individual himself/herself, with further distinctions made according to positive, neutral, or negative force connected with the use of the idiom. The major use of an idiom is then shown in the exercises where the learner sees it embedded in likely situational contexts and is asked to make distinctions as dictated by the miniature slices of life portrayed there.

A profitable and efficient approach for the learner, we feel, is to establish a ready bridge from the known German form to its English counterpart and to avoid the need to memorize an English idiom and its meaning, thus eliminating formal definitions and rules save for those areas where meaning or usage do not entire-

---

* Jürg Strässler. 1982. *Idioms in English*. Tübingen: Narr, p. 133

**Werner Koller. 1977. *Redensarten*. Tübingen: Niemeyer.

ly overlap. Therefore, where the range of application of an English idiom diverges from that of its German counterpart, the learner will find appropriate notes, explanations, and examples to help him delimit the constraints existing in English.

The workbook approach with its series of exercises to help establish and strengthen one's command of each idiom is conducive to self-study as well as to a classroom setting. The materials are programmed to permit constant review and reinforcement via the answer keys for each exercise. In addition to repeated practice modes involving the 158 primary entries in this book, the student is given 178 further English idioms related in various ways to the primary ones. All idioms are readily accessible via German and English indices at the back of the book; therefore, this workbook can serve as a reference source later. A final test covering all of the primary inventory of idioms enables the learners to confirm their ability to distinguish the appropriate idiom for the given situational context and their success in mastering these common idiomatic expressions in English. For the best way to use this workbook to that end, please see the following instructions.

Adolf E. Hieke
Universität Bayreuth

Elsa Lattey
Universität Tübingen

Acknowledgements

The work expended on putting together a workbook stands in no relation to the meager volume of the final product, the completion of which involved contributions by many of our colleagues, students, friends, typists and a circle of experts and educators. They all deserve our gratitude, but special thanks go to: Hans Borchers, Erika Duncanson, Carol Geppert-Jolly, Patricia Lech, Waltraud Mönnich, Barbara Piel.

INSTRUCTIONS

The exercises are programmed in such a way that you can work independently. All the answers are provided in the answer key in the back, and you can readily find any idiom you have come across in this workbook by looking it up in either the English or the German index. Set aside enough time to complete each exercise - including a check on the correct answers - in one and the same sitting, but leave time between units. Mark your answers in the book and check them against the answer key in the back when you have completed an entire exercise. Throughout, there is only *one* best answer for each question. Carefully go over the errors you made and determine why you might have made mistakes. Go to the trouble to re-work those portions where you have been wrong. It pays to have a clear understanding of what each idiom means and under what circumstances it occurs in conversation when you want to use it in your speech later.

Test yourself: Circle the answer of your choice (a, b, c, d) in the book; if you are not sure, mark your choices with a question mark and resolve the problems later when you check your answers against the answer key.

Idiom entries: You already know the German idioms, what they mean and how they can be used, so that now you need only to establish the bridge to their English counterparts. If the German and English idioms overlap in their common situational and grammatical use, nothing further is said. But where their range of application differs, this is pointed out. You should carefully study the notes, comments, and extensions noted below the entry. These will include references to synonyms or near synonyms, to related idioms, to semantic opposites or idioms with reverse force, and, where applicable, to "false friends", i.e. idioms which are close in form but greatly diverge in meaning. A list of symbols used in this connection appears at the end of these instructions. Once you understand the bridge between the German idiom and the corresponding English one and where the range of uses might differ, you are ready to return to the **Test yourself** section to correct the errors you may have noted there. Whenever you have difficulty doing any of the exercises in this workbook, always refer to the **Idiom entry** section. Each idiom is numbered, and you can find it again quickly. It is imperative that you trace errors or potential errors back to their source so that you will avoid them in the future.

Recognition: Here you review your understanding of each English idiom by matching it to the appropriate paraphrase. Write the phrase that best corresponds to each idiom in the space provided or circle the correct multiple choice answer. If you have been misled by one of the wrong answers, study the **Idiom entry** once more, and perhaps review its appropriate use as illustrated in the previous exercise.

Story completion: Each idiom is now used as part of a little story, and the paraphrases in parentheses are to help you write in the correct form of it in the space provided. No natural narration or conversation would contain this many idioms in close succession, of course, but the context provided allows you to work with these idioms in a very concentrated way to get to know them more quickly. Since each of the exercise types becomes a bit more difficult and requires you to make ever finer distinctions among the idioms of one unit, you should not feel discouraged if you continue to make mistakes, but always try to figure out what made you choose the wrong answer. Then you should consult the **Idiom entry** again; if necessary, you can refer to the German counterpart to help you distinguish between two English idioms you may have mixed up, since you know the German meaning best.

Situation fit: You must now discriminate among idioms according to specific situations in which they are embedded. Choose from the idiom inventory repeated for your convenience at the end of this exercise. As you check what you have entered in the spaces provided against the answer key, be sure to compare the grammatical forms as well (such as the correct tense, progressive form, pronoun reference and the like).

Do not rush through these units with undue haste and don't attempt too much at a time. You will get the idioms mixed up if you try to cope with too many of them in close succession. After you have completed Unit 9, set aside a block of time for a **Final check** of what you have learned. This test involves all the primary idioms (158) covered in this workbook, and for each question you are to pick out the right idiom from the distractors, which are taken from the same inventory. If it turns out that you have in fact been misled at times, by consulting the answer key you will find the number of the original **Idiom entry** for both the right and the wrong choices. If you have chosen a wrong answer, take the time to go back to the original entry for that *wrong* idiom, and go over its meaning and use once more. Then also return to the *right* idiom, the one you should have chosen, in the same manner, so that you can compare and contrast them one final time. It is important for you to resolve all remaining problems in this manner so that you will have a clear grasp of each idiom when you want to use it later or when you come across it in the speech of others. Do not leave this workbook until you can clearly distinguish among problematic idioms, and review those portions of the exercises which you originally had wrong or where you had question marks. The indices enable a quick check back. Idiom use is sometimes tricky, and if you take the few moments necessary for a review of difficult items, you will be more sure-footed later when you use these idioms in your active vocabulary.

It will also increase your command of a particular idiom if you return to the **Idiom entries** and go through them, making up your own little situational contexts in which you can use them naturally. If you do this in written form, your own situational use of these idioms could be checked through by your teacher or someone else who knows English well. The more often you practice the use of an idiom, the more familiar it will become, and the less you will need to refer to its German counterpart. Finally, before you "start the ball rolling," always have a dictionary handy for the many other vocabulary items which occur in the little scenes that form the backdrop for these idiom exercises.

ABBREVIATION KEY

FUT	future
IMP	imperative
NEG	negative
OP	opposite
PRES	present
PROG	progessive (or continuous) form
QUES	question
restr.	restricted to
REV	reverse (A→B : B→A)
usu.	usually

EXPLANATION OF TERMS IN IDIOM ENTRIES

Also = synonym or near synonym

See also = refers you to a related German idiom with its English correlate(s)

Note also = gives a related expression, usually in context, or an additional exemplary use of the entry

But note = indicates "watch out"; do not be misled by a similar-sounding idiom. Includes "false friends" (cf. instructions).

/ / contains an explanatory note or a reference to semantic or pragmatic domains

UNIT 1 TEST YOURSELF

1. The good thing about dealing with Joe is that you always know where you stand with him:
   a) He doesn't live high off the hog
   b) He doesn't mince words
   c) He builds castles in the air
   d) He calls the tune

2. If the department head says we've got to do it all over again, then we'll have to do it all over again, because he
   a) keeps a stiff upper lip
   b) acts on his own authority
   c) builds castles in the air
   d) calls the shots

3. There was a lot of excitement because none of us were sure how the committee would vote. But when the day came, they
   a) rested on their oars
   b) racked their brains
   c) let it dawn on them
   d) showed their true colors

4. No wonder you got your money so fast. The loan officer avoided the credit-office red tape and
   a) stuck his neck out
   b) built castles in the air
   c) acted on his own authority
   d) weighed his words

5. Although the Simmers have a very limited income, once a year, during their vacation, they
   a) go full blast
   b) rest on their oars
   c) live high off the hog
   d) take their life in their hands

6. Jack thinks that just because everybody else in the house chips in on the housework, he
   a) can rest on his oars
   b) can call the shots
   c) need not bat an eyelash
   d) can go full blast

7. Wendy really had to run to catch that train. Ultimately she
   a) didn't mince words
   b) acted on her own authority
   c) kept a stiff upper lip
   d) made it by the skin of her teeth

8. If you throw your lot in with that bunch, you may get into a lot of trouble. In fact, you'll be
    a) taking your life into your hands
    b) changing your tune
    c) acting on your own authority
    d) making yourself scarce

9. If you're foolish enough to let Max drive, you'll soon find out that you're
    a) showing your true colors
    b) making it by the skin of your teeth
    c) sticking your neck out
    d) playing it safe

10. You simply must ... as to where the key is or we're stuck here!
    a) weigh your words
    b) let it dawn on you
    c) rack your brain
    d) change your tune

11. As soon as they saw the cops coming, the whole bunch of them
    a) hightailed it out of there
    b) made themselves scarce
    c) made it by the skin of their teeth
    d) put a brave face on it

12. After he had waited an extra half hour, it finally ... that he had been stood up by his date.
    a) racked his brain
    b) dawned on him
    c) changed his tune
    d) showed his true colors

13. The reason why this man will never get anywhere in life is that all he ever does is
    a) live high off the hog
    b) not bat an eyelash
    c) build castles in the air
    d) not mince words

14. Cheryl was a cool thief. When the manager accused her of shoplifting, she
    a) stuck her neck out
    b) kept a stiff upper lip
    c) put a brave face on it
    d) didn't bat an eyelash

15. Bill's in-laws came to visit so rarely that when they did come, he managed to
    a) put a brave face on it
    b) make it by the skin of his teeth
    c) call the shots
    d) make himself scarce

16. I doubt that Jean and the kids will try to cross the Continental Divide after nightfall. She'll stay overnight in Taos and
    a) let it dawn on her
    b) play it safe
    c) rest on her oars
    d) hightail it out of there

17. Wendell was a real sport. All through the ordeal, he
    a) called the tune
    b) called the shots
    c) took his life in his hands
    d) kept a stiff upper lip

18. Boy, I don't know about our kids these days. Whenever Mom calls for help with the dishes, they
    a) rest on their oars
    b) make themselves scarce
    c) put a brave face on it
    d) go full blast

19. We'll let Joe handle the negotiations. He's highly respected and is good at
    a) calling the tune
    b) not mincing words
    c) showing his colors
    d) sticking his neck out

20. If the kids keep railroading her like they do, she'll soon be forced to
    a) call the shots
    b) change her tune
    c) rack her brain
    d) play it safe

21. The President's speech caused the ticker tape at the Stock Exchange to
    a) live high off the hog
    b) hightail it out of there
    c) call the tune
    d) go full blast

22. In such a sensitive situation, we must all take care
    a) to weigh our words
    b) to take our lives into our hands
    c) not to bat an eyelash
    d) to rack our brains

UNIT 1   IDIOM ENTRIES AND USAGE
Focus on the Individual (non-negative)

1.1   *kein Blatt vor den Mund nehmen*

     ** not mince words **   PROG rare

     * Also: not pull one's punches
     OP: weigh one's words
     See also: jdm reinen Wein einschenken (4.17)
                   kein Hehl aus etwas machen (7.12)

1.2   *alle Fäden in der Hand halten/haben*

     ** call the shots **

     * Also: have everything under one's thumb /*authoritarian*/
     But note: pull strings /*secretly exercise influence*/
                   I don't care which way we go. You call the shots!
     See also: fest im Sattel sitzen (6.16)
                   den Ton angeben (1.19)

1.3   *Farbe bekennen*

     ** show one's (true) colors **

     But note: When she switched majors, he followed suit.

1.4   *etwas auf eigene Faust tun*

     ** act on one's own authority **

1.5   *auf großem Fuß leben*

     ** live high off the hog **

     * Also: live in (grand) style
                   live in the lap of luxury
                   live the life of Riley

1.6   *die Hände in den Schoß legen*

     ** rest on one's oars ** /*pause*/

     But note: rest on one's laurels /*do nothing more*/
                 twiddle one's thumbs /*do nothing*/

1.7   *mit heiler Haut davonkommen*

     ** make it by the skin of one's teeth **

     But note: save one's own skin

1.8   *seine Haut zu Markte tragen*

     ** take one's life in(to) one's hands ** /*acknowledge risks*/
     See next entry.

1.9 *Kopf und Kragen riskieren*

   ** stick one's neck out ** /invite risk/

   * Also: risk one's hide
                   neck
   See previous entry.

1.10 *sich den Kopf zerbrechen*

   ** rack one's brain(s) (over something) **

   * Also: beat one's brains out
   But note: *Zerbrechen Sie sich darüber nicht den Kopf!* =
              Don't worry about that!
              Don't rack your brain (over it) = Don't exert yourself unduly!

1.11 *Leine ziehen*

   ** hightail it out of there **

   Ex.   We hightailed it out of the schoolyard.
   IMP: Beat it!
   But note: I pulled strings to get you the job.
   See also: *sich aus dem Staube machen* (1.18)

1.12 *jdm geht ein Licht auf*

   ** it dawns on s.o. **

   QUES: Is it beginning to dawn on you?
   FUT: When he reads this, he'll see the light.
   * Also: (finally) see the light
   Note also: They were quick/slow on the uptake.

1.13 *Luftschlösser bauen*

   ** build castles in the air **
                        Spain **

   Note also: That's just a pipedream!
   But note: build a house of cards /on a poor foundation/

1.14 *keine Miene verziehen*

   ** not bat an eye(lash) **

   * Also: be (as) cool as a cucumber
   But note: without batting an eyelash = *ohne mit der Wimper zu zucken*

1.15 *gute Miene zum bösen Spiel machen*

   ** put a brave face on it **

   subject usu. 3rd. person

1.16 *auf Nummer sicher gehen*

   ** play it safe **

1.17 *die Ohren steif halten*

** keep a stiff upper lip **

usu. IMP
*Also: keep one's chin up
IMP also: Hang in there! /in parting/
See also: sich nicht unterkriegen lassen (4.15)

1.18 *sich aus dem Staube machen*

** make oneself scarce **

* Also: take to one's heels
           make tracks
           head for the hills
But note: Don't make yourself so scarce. = Come and visit us more often.
See also: Leine ziehen (1.11)

1.19 *den Ton angeben*

** call the tune **

* Also: set the fashion /people, objects/
OP: dance to s.o. (else)'s tune
See also: alle Fäden in der Hand halten (1.2)

1.20 *eine andere Tonart anschlagen*

** change one's tune **

* Also: get tough with s.o.

1.21 *auf vollen Touren laufen*

** go full blast **

usu. PROG

1.22 *die Zunge im Zaum halten*

** weigh one's words **

* Also: mind one's p's and q's /speech or action/
OP: not mince words
But note: Mind your tongue! = Watch your language!
           Hold your tongue! = Be quiet!

* * * * * * *

1.23 *die Ärmel hochkrempeln*

** roll up one's sleeves **

1.24 *wieder auf die Beine kommen*

** get back on one's feet **

1.25 *den Gürtel enger schnallen*

** tighten one's belt **

1.26 *seine Haut retten*

** save one's skin

UNIT 1 RECOGNITION

1. not mince words   _____
2. call the tune   _____
3. change one's tune   _____
4. weigh one's words   _____

    a) carefully think about what one says
    b) guide the group
    c) say very little
    d) set the tone
    e) behave differently
    f) openly express an opinion

5. show one's true colors   _____
6. not bat an eyelash   _____
7. put a brave face on it   _____
8. keep a stiff upper lip   _____

    a) raise the flag
    b) bear adversity
    c) reveal one's attitude
    d) show no reaction
    e) smile broadly
    f) not lose heart

9. live high off the hog   _____
10. hightail it out of there _____
11. build castles in the air _____
12. go full blast   _____

    a) aim for the heights
    b) maintain maximum activity
    c) enjoy luxury
    d) enjoy adventure
    e) have unrealistic goals
    f) run away

13. call the shots
    a) announce a golf game
    b) give orders
    c) play billiards
    d) work as a telephone operator

14. act on one's own authority
    a) finance a play oneself
    b) be in charge
    c) make decisions independently
    d) be told what to do

15. rest on one's oars
    a) sleep on board a boat
    b) pause for a while
    c) achieve success
    d) give up

16. make it by the skin of one's teeth
    a) invest a great deal
    b) do on one's own
    c) barely escape
    d) risk one's career

17. take one's life into one's hands
    a) take care of s.o.
    b) get a new start
    c) face danger
    d) commit suicide

18. stick one's neck out
    a) take a risk
    b) act ostentatiously
    c) aim at a position of authority
    d) check on the weather

19. rack one's brain
    a) think hard
    b) have a headache
    c) study for an examination
    d) undergo torture

20. it dawns on s.o.
    a) morning comes
    b) one awakens
    c) one realizes s.t.
    d) it is difficult to understand

21. play it safe
    a) score a run
    b) bet hesitantly
    c) help rescue s.t.
    d) not take any risks

22. make oneself scarce
    a) remain alone
    b) chase others off
    c) depart conveniently
    d) build a wall around oneself

UNIT 1 STORY COMPLETION

When talking about Big Bad John, it won't do to _____ _____ (speak too considerately of him), so here is the full story on why that crook was so lucky for such a long time. As leader of his gang, of course, John was used to _____ _____ _____ (giving orders); nobody doubted that he was boss. He could always make his men _____ _____ _____ _____ (reveal their attitude), and so they never _____ _____ _____ _____ _____ (made decisions) if they wanted to stay on his good side. After all, he made it possible for all of them to _____ _____ _____ _____ _____ (enjoy luxury), even if he made them work hard and never gave them a chance to _____ _____ _____ _____ (relax) and loaf.

Every once in a while one of his gang would be pulled in by the police, but John was too smart for them, and always got away, though he sometimes just _____ _____ _____ _____ _____ _____ _____ (escaped narrowly).

Often he had to _____ _____ _____ _____ _____ _____ (risk everything) to make his get-away. But somehow he always managed, no matter how much he _____ _____ _____ _____ (took a chance). If he got into a tight corner, he always found a way to _____ _____ _____ _____ _____ (leave hurriedly) with the cops in hot pursuit, _____ _____ _____ (thinking hard) how they might trap him in the end.

Finally _____ _____ _____ _____ (they realized) that he had to have an inside informer, somebody who might be lured by the promise of reward, somebody with dreams involving lots of money. All they had to do was to watch for someone on the force who tended to _____ _____ _____ _____ _____ (dream wild dreams), who would accept bribes without _____ _____ _____ (compunction). But the police commissioner couldn't find that man and Big Bad John kept getting away. The commissioner received much public criticism and had to _____ _____ _____ _____ _____ (appear undisturbed) whenever he stepped up to a TV camera. He was sure that John couldn't _____ _____ _____ (avoid taking chances) forever and would have to take chances sometimes. So when it came to contact with the public, he _____ _____ _____ _____ _____ (acted brave) and _____ _____ _____ (avoided attention) as much as possible. He hoped to give John a false sense of security by making him think that he still

_____ _____ _____ (was in control) and then to pounce on him as soon as his guard was down. If he could nab Big Bad John and lock him away behind bars, that would soon cut the crook down to size and make him _____ _____ _____ (act differently) and cry for mercy.

The commissioner had time on his side, and when the moment finally came and John was careless for an instant, he and his men swooped in, caught him, rushed him to headquarters and kept _____ _____ _____ (working at top speed) until they had caught up with the last man of Big Bad John's old gang. It had been a long and gruesome effort, but the commissioner had succeeded and he made it a point to escort Big Bad John to the Federal Penitentiary personally. Perhaps he can be excused for not carefully _____ _____ _____ (watching his language) as he sent him off to 25 years in jail. At any rate, he told him good-by using language he just couldn't have picked up in Sunday School.

* * * * *

UNIT 1   SITUATION FIT

1. Look, honey, regardless of what happens tonight, remember he's my boss, so please don't lose your temper.

   Don't you bet on it. I am sick of _____ whenever we're over at their house and have to listen to that old bore, and some day I'm going to explode. Just wait.

2. All right, Tommy, for the last time, when did you last see the car keys?

   There's no need to scream at me, Dad. I'm _____ as it is, and you're just making me nervous. Believe me, I don't want to hike all the way back to the lake either.

3. Here comes Harry. I want to have a word with him about last night. This partying has got to stop. I didn't sleep a wink, and I'm about to let him have it.

Please wait until tomorrow before you talk to him. By then you'll have cooled off. You know how you have to _____ with him if you want to avoid a regular fight. He's just as hot-headed as you are.

4. I could use a bit more leeway in assigning the workload to the staff. Any objections, Henry?

   No, that's fine with me. It's better for company morale anyway if one person _____, and you are responsible for the day-to-day operation of the company in any case.

5. Hi there! can I give you a ride home in my dreamboat?

   Are you kidding? If I got into that wreck of yours I'd be _____ _____. The way you drive, I feel safer walking.

6. Did you see that fancy yacht in Leeman's driveway just now? Did he flip his lid or what?

   Oh, haven't you heard? He has actually won the big prize in the New York State Lottery, and now he's _____, that lucky dog.

7. Well, take it easy, and have a good trip. I don't know how I'll get through these two months, though. It's an awfully long time for you to be gone.

   So long, dear, and don't count the time. Just _____ and it won't seem so bad, you'll see. Be a brave girl. There you are.

8. I can just see it: a split-level with a sundeck down by the ocean, our own sailboat in the cove below, and the two of us in the sun all weekend.

   Oh, Ricky, stop _____ and be realistic for a change. For a start, how about you and me finishing high school?

9. It's not that I don't appreciate your good advice, doctor, but I've got a company to run, you know, and ...

   You underestimate the gravity of your situation, Mr. Clark, so I won't _____: What you've just had is a small heart attack. You keep up those 16-hour workdays, and the next one may be fatal.

10. Hey, where are you going? I haven't even gotten my first bite. And this fishing spot is perfect, isn't it?

Forget it, Harry, and get your gear together fast. Here comes the game warden. He's already spotted us, so we'd better _____, trout or no trout.

11. Come on, I just have to tie these suitcases to the roof-rack and then we can get going. It's not that long a trip.

Yes, but it looks like rain. Better _____ and cover them with a tarp, just in case. It would be a shame to ruin our luggage.

12. Welcome home, Steve. Well, how did it go? Did you manage to talk the boss into a promotion?

Forget it. Not only did he turn me down flat, but when I kept insisting, he stopped being Mr. Nice Guy and _____ from one moment to the next and turned quite ugly. It was a nightmare.

13. It's really discouraging, I tell you. I've been looking for a job for so long I'm about ready to join the Army.

What, and _____ as soon as there's trouble? With the political situation the way it is, you'd be taking terrible chances. No, stay home and keep looking until you find another office job.

14. Now we'd like to hear from you, Mr. Parks. Can we count on you to meet the production schedule?

If we can _____ for the entire month, there won't be a problem. Let's just hope none of the assembly lines break down.

15. Do we have a public statement by the senator on how he stands on nuclear power plants?

No, he's been very close-mouthed about it, but he'll have to _____ _____ soon. The congressional committee meets next week and he'll have to take a position then.

16. Guess what: Ginny's asked me to help her with her homework again. I spend more time over at her house these days, and her work isn't really that bad. Sometimes I think she just makes all this up.

    I wondered how long it would take before _____ that it's not exactly your "C" grade average that she's interested in.

17. Where did the boys disappear to all of a sudden? I was just about to show them how to work the post-hole digger.

    As soon as you mentioned putting up the new fence, they knew it would mean work, and so they _____. I just saw them sneak out of the front door, so I'm afraid you're way too late.

18. Charlie Company is asking for permission to go on an all-night forced march, captain, unless you have other orders.

    In this weather? Tell Lieutenant Levot I leave it up to his judgement, but if he goes through with it, he is _____ entirely. It's about time he assumes some responsibility.

19. How did you do on the math test?

    I've got to do a heck of a lot better from now on if I want to pass that course. Would you believe I got 40% wrong on that test? Just _____. Boy, was that close!

20. How did Joe take the bad news that Maryanne is dating another guy now?

    He really kept himself under control when he found out and didn't _____, but it was obvious nevertheless that he was doing everything to keep from crying.

21. Listen, we've been painting all morning, and I need a break. How about having a cool beer over there in the shade?

    Oh, watch out, the foreman just drove up. It's definitely the wrong time to _____, or he'll get the wrong idea. Let's keep at it until he's gone again.

22. Don't even mention his name to me. I'm sick of St. Laurent. Everywhere I turn, it's St. Laurent this, and St. Laurent that.

   Might as well face it, when it comes to fashion, he _____ _____, and you'd do well to reckon with him from now on if you want to stay in business.

Idioms to choose from:

not mince words
call the shots
show one's (true) colors
act on one's own authority
live high off the hog
rest on one's oars
make it by the skin of one's teeth
take one's life in one's hands
stick one's neck out
rack one's brain
hightail it out of there
it dawns on s.o.
build castles in the air
not bat an eye(lash)
put a brave face on it
play it safe
keep a stiff upper lip
make oneself scarce
call the tune
change one's tune
go full blast
weigh one's words

UNIT 2 TEST YOURSELF

1. Don't even try. There's no chance that you'll persuade me, not even if
    a) you laugh up your sleeve
    b) you talk yourself hoarse
    c) you get out of line
    d) you blow your stack

2. Bill couldn't change what had happened although he ... in remorse.
    a) beat his breast
    b) flew off the handle
    c) sailed under false colors
    d) fell by the wayside

3. When the heavy vase fell off the bookcase onto Mary's head, she
    a) adorned herself with borrowed plumes
    b) was on the skids
    c) fell by the wayside
    d) saw stars

4. The puzzle was beyond me. But when even my clever sister wasn't able to solve it, I couldn't help
    a) beating my breast
    b) laughing up my sleeve
    c) giving myself airs
    d) howling with the pack

5. Don't you believe that Harry designed the bathing suit collection all by himself! I'm sure he's
    a) talking Jim's ear off
    b) adorning himself with borrowed plumes
    c) going on the warpath
    d) howling with the pack

6. Melissa is not to be trusted. To get people on her side she often
    a) sails under false colors
    b) talks herself hoarse
    c) blows her top
    d) goes on the warpath

7. "I'm going to give up my studies. I'll never pass the exam." "Don't be so negative. If you ... now, you'll never know whether you could have made it or not."
    a) fly off the handle
    b) kick the bucket
    c) see stars
    d) throw in the towel

8. When those unruly kids pulled my neighbor's wash off the line as they ran through his garden, he
   a) beat his breast
   b) blew his stack
   c) ended up on the rocks
   d) talked their ear off

9. The old bum down the block slipped on the ice and was hurt so badly that he
   a) fell by the wayside
   b) kicked the bucket
   c) threw in the towel
   d) ended up on the rocks

10. When her neighbor got her out of bed in the middle of the night for the third time this week for no good reason, Maria really
    a) flew off the handle
    b) got out of line
    c) ended up on the rocks
    d) gave herself airs

11. After years of putting up with his teammate's vindictive schemes, Jason finally decided to ... and fight back.
    a) give himself airs
    b) be on the skids
    c) go on the warpath
    d) blow his top

12. Whenever I visit my neighbors, it takes me a long time to break away. Both of them
    a) talk themselves hoarse
    b) adorn themselves with borrowed plumes
    c) talk your ear off
    d) howl with the pack

13. If Luise doesn't watch her drinking, she'll ... before long.
    a) see stars
    b) howl with the pack
    c) get out of line
    d) be on the skids

14. Everybody's trying hard, but I'm afraid we'll never achieve a unified front. One of us is always
    a) getting out of line
    b) flying off the handle
    c) going on the warpath
    d) throwing in the towel

15. Robert thinks he's something special. He's always ... and treating the rest of us like dirt.
    a) beating his breast
    b) giving himself airs
    c) laughing up his sleeve
    d) sailing under false colors

16. When Susan and Charlie became more interested in their careers than in each other, their marriage soon

    a) kicked the bucket
    b) fell by the wayside
    c) ended up on the rocks
    d) saw stars

17. When his company had to make economy cut-backs, Edgar's chances for promotion

    a) kicked the bucket
    b) ended up on the rocks
    c) fell by the wayside
    d) were on the skids

18. You can't ever expect Harriet to take a stand on an issue. She always waits until the trend is established and then she

    a) talks herself hoarse
    b) throws in the towel
    c) goes on the warpath
    d) howls with the pack

* * * * *

UNIT 2   IDIOM ENTRIES AND USAGE
Focus on the Individual (negative)

2.1   *sich den Mund in Fransen reden*

    ** **talk oneself hoarse** **

    * Also: talk one's head off
                  talk oneself blue in the face
    See also: jdm ein Loch in den Bauch reden (2.12)

2.2   *sich an die Brust schlagen*

    ** **beat one's breast** **

2.3   *die Engel im Himmel pfeifen/singen hören*

    ** **see stars** **

2.4   *sich ins Fäustchen lachen*

    ** **laugh up one's sleeve** **

2.5   *sich mit fremden Federn schmücken*

    ** **adorn oneself with borrowed plumes** **

2.6   *unter falscher Flagge segeln*

    ** **sail under false colors** **

2.7   *die Flinte ins Korn werfen*

    ** **throw in the towel** **

    * Also: strike one's colors

2.8   *Gift und Galle spucken*

　　**blow one's stack **
　　　　　　　top **

　　See also: aus der Haut fahren (2.10)

2.9   *ins Gras beißen*

　　**kick the bucket **

　　* Also: bite the dust

2.10 *aus der Haut fahren*

　　**fly off the handle **

　　* Also: lose one's temper
　　　　　　　vent one's rage (on s.o.)
　　OP: remain cool as a cucumber
　　See also: Gift und Galle spucken (2.8)

2.11 *das Kriegsbeil ausgraben*

　　**go on the warpath **

　　* Also: pick a quarrel
　　　　　　　be spoiling for a fight
　　OP: bury the hatchet

2.12 *jdm ein Loch in den Bauch reden*

　　**talk s.o.'s ear off **

　　See also: sich den Mund in Fransen reden (2.1)

2.13 *unter die Räder kommen*

　　**be on the skids ** /process/

　　* Also: go to the dogs /result/
　　See also: Schiffbruch erleiden (2.16)

2.14 *aus der Reihe tanzen*

　　**get out of line **

　　* Also: break rank
　　OP: toe the line
　　But note: go it alone /independently/

2.15 *auf dem hohen Roß sitzen / sich aufs hohe Roß setzen*

　　**give oneself airs **

　　* Also: get on one's high horse
　　NEG IMP: Get (down) off your high horse!

2.16 *Schiffbruch erleiden*

　　**end up on the rocks **

　　See also: unter die Räder kommen (2.13)

2.17 *auf der Strecke bleiben*

   ** fall by the wayside **
   ** drop **

   But note: stay on the track of /pursue/

2.18 *mit den Wölfen heulen*

   ** howl with the pack **

   * Also: swim with the tide
   But note: *man muß mit den Wölfen heulen* = when in Rome do as the Romans do

* * * * * * *

2.19 *sich den Hals brechen*

   ** break one's neck **

2.20 *aus der Rolle fallen*

   ** fall out of character **

2.21 *das Handtuch werfen*

   ** throw in the towel (cf. 2.7) **

* * * * *

UNIT 2 RECOGNITION

1. sail under false colors _____
2. blow one's stack _____
3. end up on the rocks _____
4. give oneself airs _____

   a) commit suicide
   b) express one's anger
   c) act deceptively
   d) fail in life
   e) keep the window open
   f) act condescendingly
   g) be shipwrecked

5. be on the skids _____
6. get out of line _____
7. fall by the wayside _____
8. kick the bucket _____

   a) fail to conform
   b) stray from the path
   c) be exhausted
   d) drop out
   e) die
   f) be likely to go under

9. talk oneself hoarse
   a) discuss angrily
   b) talk too much
   c) talk oneself into a rage
   d) try strongly to persuade

10. beat one's breast
    a) play the leader
    b) listen to one's heart
    c) boast about achievements
    d) blame oneself

11. see stars
    a) go to the theater
    b) be knocked dizzy
    c) study astronomy
    d) have good weather

12. laugh up one's sleeve
    a) laugh maliciously
    b) snicker out loud
    c) delight in someone else's predicament
    d) laugh at someone

13. adorn oneself with borrowed plumes
    a) spend someone else's money
    b) dress up in someone else's clothes
    c) claim someone else's achievements
    d) follow in someone else's footsteps

14. throw in the towel
    a) give up a fight
    b) add something for good measure
    c) take a bath
    d) insult someone

15. fly off the handle
    a) lose one's temper
    b) stumble and fall
    c) get ready for take-off
    d) break something by force

16. go on the warpath
    a) invite a quarrel
    b) walk in single file
    c) travel an Indian trail
    d) start a fighting campaign

17. talk someone's ear off
    a) bore someone
    b) scold someone vehemently
    c) annoy someone with one's chatter
    d) deafen with loud noise

18. howl with the pack
    a) get thrown to the wolves
    b) do as one is told when convenient
    c) follow the lead of others when opportune
    d) shout approval

UNIT 2 STORY COMPLETION

The plaintiff plainly stated that you hit him so hard that for an instant he _____ _____ *(nearly lost consciousness)*. You can _____ _____ _____ *(talk and talk)*, defendant, but it will be in vain, for the court is well aware of your attempt to _____ _____ _____ *(show remorse)* in the hope of avoiding a fine. No one can fast-talk his way out of a charge here, or be given a chance to _____ _____ _____ _____ *(make fun of things)* at the expense of justice, I assure you. The court particularly resents the use of terminology such as that sometimes employed by would-be lawyers. You will fail to impress us with your attempt to _____ _____ _____ _____ _____ *(claim undue credit)*. Your record already shows that you tend to _____ _____ _____ _____ *(make pretenses)*, so you may as well stop the charade now and _____ _____ _____ _____ *(give up)*. Let us get back to the facts instead: During last night's altercation at the Frothy Mug, the doorman testified, you, as he put it, _____ _____ _____ *(got mad)* when you weren't admitted, and you threatened his life. He accuses you of bragging that your punch was powerful enough to make him _____ _____ _____ *(die)*. Then the doorman _____ _____ _____ _____ *(lost his temper)* in turn, perhaps unwisely, but then his job constantly confronts him with drunks trying to force their way onto the premises. The doorman further testified that you _____ _____ _____ _____ *(talked too much)*, to use his words, and that you tried to gain entrance by shoving and pushing him around. He further stated that such harrassment by customers is frequent enough to make anyone _____ _____ _____ _____ *(fighting mad)*. Such exchanges automatically lead one to negative thinking, and every intoxicated troublemaker then appears to _____ _____ _____ _____ *(lose out in life)* and beyond redemption. Customer relations in the gastronomy business are difficult and full of conflict. As to the present case, it is clear that you, the defendant, _____ _____ _____ _____ *(exceeded your bounds)* and in general aggravated the situation by acting superior and _____ _____ _____ *(pretending to be something better)*. Statements such as the one that bouncers inevitably _____ _____ _____ _____ *(come to no good)* only worsen the situation. It is doubtful that doormen _____ _____ _____ _____ *(become losers in life)* more often than their patrons inside, and so your hot-winded protest appears to be a misplaced attempt to _____ _____ _____ _____ *(go along with everybody else)*. Six days or a two-hundred dollar fine. Court adjourned.

UNIT 2 SITUATION FIT

1. "How come Mr. Baker left town so suddenly?"

   "He was trying to establish himself as a chiropractor, but the Department of Health discovered that he was _____. He doesn't have any medical training at all."

2. "Hey, Wilma, guess who finally _____?"

   "Well, if it's left you so unmoved, it must be that old mechanic down at the plant whose retirement you've been longing for all these years!"

3. "Mrs. Brett, the woman down on the first floor, was here trying to enlist me in her ladies' aid group. The fact that I work full time and have a household and two kids to take care of didn't deter her one bit. She kept telling me about all their activities and how well I'd fit in and simply wouldn't give up even though I'd plainly said no."

   "Oh, yes, I know her. You can't let her get her foot in the door or she'll _____, no matter what the topic."

4. "I wonder how it could come to this. Wilfred has been suspended from school for cheating. I thought he was such a good student."

   "That's the problem. Apparently he's gotten that reputation by _____. It's not the first time he's plagiarized a report—it's just the first time he got caught at it."

5. "I don't care what the rest of you decide to do. I'm going to Washington this weekend."

   "That's precisely what I've been complaining about! We're supposed to be a team, and a team can only function when everybody pulls together. We're scheduled to play an exhibition game in Boston and can't have individual members suddenly deciding to go off on their own. I've had enough of your _____. Either you come with us to Boston or you're off the team."

6. "The coach has been complaining about our attendance at practice again."

"That doesn't surprise me. If we showed up for orchestra rehearsals as irregularly as you do for football practice, our conductor would virtually _____, and he would see to it that our weekend passes get cancelled, you can be sure of that."

7. "Sheila and Henry have split up."

"That's no surprise. Their interests are so different, and one or the other was constantly running off -- not to mention running around -- on his or her own, that their marriage was bound to _____ before long."

8. "I'm so upset. Never in a million years would I do anything to hurt Lucy and now it's my fault that she's lost her job."

"Well, _____ isn't going to make it any better. What you should do is actively try to help her find another one."

9. "I really feel sorry for Mabel. She tried so hard to keep up with her college friends."

"I know, but I think it's largely their fault. At first they pushed her beyond her capabilities and then when she collapsed under the burden, they simply let her _____. Fine friends they are."

10. "How was work today?"

"Infuriating. The computer was constantly out of order because of a short circuit and then somebody in another department had the nerve to insinuate that my program was causing the difficulties. Did I ever _____ when I heard that!"

11. "Why is Cornelia acting so smug?"

"It turned out that the supervisor who's been getting on her back about efficiency all the time made a big mistake herself and cost the company thousands of dollars. The supervisor's been reprimanded and Cornelia has taken over 'accounts receivable'. It's only natural that she's _____ _____ now."

12. "Have you seen Lou lately? He looks awful."

"Yes, I know, It's really sad. He lost his job and then his wife ran off with another guy and now he's being evicted from his apartment. And so he really _____."

13. "That child is incorrigible, Amy. His room is a sight. I don't know how he can stand to live in such a pig-sty."

"I know, George. It's really depressing. Believe me, I _____ _____ but it's no use. He nods and says o.k., but then does just as he pleases."

14. "Mom, I've had it with Burt. I never want to see him again."

"What happened, Janie?"

"I used to think he had ideals. At least he would stand up for what he felt was right. But as soon as his cronies voice a different opinion, he just _____ _____ and forgets all that he believes in."

15. "Why so blue?"

"I've offered my new novel to three publishers already and everybody has turned it down."

"But that's no reason to _____. There are plenty more publishing houses in this city."

16. "Will you please see to it that my evening dress is pressed and laid out by 7:30? I'll want to change and be down for dinner promptly at 8."

"Look, you needn't _____ here. This is an extremely casual household and you'd do best to behave accordingly if you want to fit in."

17. "What's so funny?"

   "You know that unfriendly guy down the block? The one who always complains about everything and never lets the kids cross his property? The kids decided to get back at him and stuck a pin in his doorbell when he was working way up in the attic. If that didn't make him _____. In fact, he tripped all over himself trying to get downstairs to make the noise stop."

18. "What's the matter with you?"

   "I guess I'm a bit dizzy and weak in the knees. When that carton of books fell off the shelf and hit me on the head, for a moment I _____ _____ and I'm still not completely over it."

Idioms to choose from:

end up on the rocks
see stars
howl with the pack
kick the bucket
go on the warpath
talk s.o.'s ear off
talk oneself hoarse
get out of line
laugh up one's sleeve
throw in the towel
beat one's breast
give oneself airs
fly off the handle
be on the skids
sail under false colors
fall by the wayside
blow one's stack
adorn oneself with borrowed plumes

UNIT 3 TEST YOURSELF

1. I've been in the country for such a short time that I'd sure be grateful if you could
    a) lend me a helping hand
    b) stick up for me
    c) go to bat for me
    d) give me some moral support

2. I have a notion that Jackie will soon have a new boyfriend. I notice that she's sure
    a) telling Jim things in a roundabout way
    b) throwing dust in Jim's eyes
    c) making eyes at Jim
    d) sweeping Jim off his feet

3. It certainly is too bad that John has dandruff. I wish somebody would take the courage to
    a) throw dust in his eyes
    b) tell him in a roundabout way
    c) lend him a helping hand
    d) stand up for him

4. The only reason they could ever have gotten away with it was that they ... from the start.
    a) didn't harm a hair on my head
    b) made eyes at me
    c) went to bat for me
    d) threw dust in my eyes

5. His new position gives him such authority that from now on we'll have to
    a) treat him with kid gloves
    b) give him moral support
    c) stand up for him
    d) tell him things in a roundabout way

6. Actually she's quite devious, but she looks as if she couldn't
    a) throw dust in anybody's eyes
    b) harm a hair on anybody's head
    c) treat anyone with kid gloves
    d) sweep anybody off their feet

7. I took only one look at her and right away she
    a) lent me a helping hand
    b) made eyes at me
    c) went to bat for me
    d) swept me off my feet

8. At one point they even wanted to fire Frank, but luckily, his boss really
   a) went to bat for him
   b) gave him moral support
   c) didn't harm a hair on his head
   d) lent him a helping hand

9. Now that your wife has experienced such a setback, you simply must
   a) handle her with kid gloves
   b) make eyes at her
   c) give her moral support
   d) sweep her off her feet

10. If I get into real trouble, can I depend on you
    a) not to harm a hair on my head?
    b) to tell me everything in a roundabout way?
    c) to stand up for me?
    d) to handle me with kid gloves?

* * * * *

UNIT 3 IDIOM ENTRIES AND USAGE
Interaction of Individuals (positive)

3.1 jdm unter die Arme greifen

   ** lend s.o. a helping hand **

   QUES and IMP without "helping"
   But note: lend s.o. a hand /short-term aid/
              give

3.2 jdm schöne Augen machen

   ** make eyes at s.o. **

   But note: give s.o. the eye /has both positive and negative readings/

3.3 jdm etwas durch die Blume sagen

   ** tell s.o. something in a roundabout way **

   ** break it to s.o. gently ** /news/

   ** give s.o. a gentle hint ** /etiquette, etc./

   But note: I hear through the grapevine that ... /= gossip/
             put it mildly /understate/
             give s.o. a broad hint (4.18)

3.4 jdm blauen Dunst vormachen

   ** throw dust in s.o.'s eyes **

   See also: jdn hinters Licht führen (5.17)

3.5 jdn behandeln wie ein rohes Ei

   ** treat s.o. with kid gloves **
   ** handle

   OP: ride roughshod over s.o.

3.6 *jdm kein Haar krümmen*

    ** **not harm a hair on s.o.'s head** **
        hurt

    Note also: He's the sort of person who wouldn't hurt a fly.

3.7 *jdm den Kopf verdrehen*

    ** **sweep s.o. off his/her feet** **

    * Also: turn s.o.'s head

3.8 *für jdn eine Lanze brechen*

    ** **go to bat for s.o.** **

    See also: jdm die Stange halten (3.10)

3.9 *jdm den Rücken stärken*

    ** **give s.o. moral support** **

3.10 *jdm die Stange halten*

    ** **stand up for s.o.** **
    ** **stick**

    But note: take s.o.'s side /*in an argument*/
    See also: für jdn eine Lanze brechen (3.8)

* * * * * * *

3.11 *jdm wieder auf die Beine helfen*

    ** **help s.o. back on(to) his/her feet** **

3.12 *das Eis brechen*

    ** **break the ice** **

3.13 *jdn beim Wort nehmen*

    ** **take s.o. at his/her word** **

                     * * * * *

UNIT 3 RECOGNITION

1. lend s.o. a helping hand
   a) help s.o. back on his feet
   b) pull s.o.'s leg
   c) provide s.o. with assistance
   d) interfere in s.o.'s affairs

2. make eyes at s.o.
   a) look at s.o. with admiration
   b) make s.o. up
   c) keep an eye an s.o.
   d) watch out for someone

3. break it to s.o. gently
   a) congratulate s.o.
   b) announce an achievement
   c) send s.o. flowers
   d) soften unpleasant news

4. throw dust in s.o.'s eyes
   a) smoke a lot
   b) produce a blurred image
   c) pretend to help s.o.
   d) mislead s.o.

5. treat s.o. with kid gloves
   a) be very polite with s.o.
   b) tread on delicate ground
   c) keep one's hands off s.o.
   d) not touch s.o. with a 10-ft. pole

6. not harm a hair on s.o.'s head
   a) be overly polite
   b) treat nicely
   c) encourage neatness in s.o.
   d) not say anything bad about s.o.

7. sweep s.o. off their feet
   a) cause s.o. to look around
   b) beat s.o. up
   c) carry s.o. over the doorstep
   d) overwhelm s.o.

8. go to bat for s.o.
   a) start an offensive
   b) come to blows
   c) put down one's arms
   d) defend s.o. against others

9. give s.o. moral support
   a) encourage s.o. to go on
   b) plot with s.o.
   c) agree with s.o.
   d) push s.o. to the wall

10. stick up for s.o.
    a) act as assistant to s.o.
    b) offer s.o. aid
    c) steal for s.o.
    d) give s.o. support

* * * * *

UNIT 3 STORY COMPLETION

My dear Harold, I know you're not in the habit of _____ anyone _____ _____ _____ (assisting), but could you tear yourself away from the picture window long enough to help finish the paint job this afternoon? I can see from here that that devastating blond Julie Crypton is out there, but I assure you that *she* can't see you _____ _____ _____ _____ (ogling her), which is just as well, because you look as if you're baring your teeth at the front lawn. Once you have quite recovered from your exertions, I think it would be high time for somebody to _____ _____ _____ _____ _____ (tell you kindly) that your courting days are over. No, no, don't try to _____ _____ _____ _____ _____ (fool me) with another round of your windy excuses. So far I have made every effort to be understanding while you putter through your midlife crisis, but your foolishness in connection with that Crypton girl is so blatant that I can't overlook it any longer. So don't expect me to go on _____ _____ _____ _____ _____ (being gentle with you), my dear aging Harold. You know I wouldn't _____ _____ _____ _____ _____ _____ (hurt anyone), but if you don't wake up to the fact that the days when you managed to _____ *young women* _____ _____ _____ (enchant) ended with me, I'll sock you. Get that, you old lecher? In the end it is always the same, I've got to run around the neighborhood making amends for your foolishness. So if you expect me to ever _____ _____ _____ _____ _____ (support you) again in the future, you come over here in a hurry and grab that paint-brush. That's better, Harold. I'm sorry I had to be so blunt with you just now, and you do realize, don't you, that you can always rely on me when you need someone to _____ _____ _____ _____ (encourage you) in everything you do, everything but further displays of amorous advances that only frighten the young women in the neighborhood. As long as you expect me to _____ _____ _____ _____ (protect your reputation) vis-à-vis the neighbors, Harold, you ...

Yuck, Harold, now look what you've done! Whatever made you paint my cheek green, for crying out loud?

* * * * *

UNIT 3   SITUATION FIT

1. I hear Jack Witting is stopping over on his way home tonight. He couldn't have picked a more inopportune time.

   Oh, my god, don't let him know you're upset. I beg you to _____ _____. I've got to stay on good terms with him, because he may be my new boss, you know.

2. All right, all right, skip the rest. I get the message. Now, what do you want from me?

   I'm sorry if I seem to pressure you, but I did in fact want to ask you to

_____ at next week's tenure board meeting. There's going to be a lot of argument, as there always is, and it would be good to have someone there representing my interests.

3. I hear that Mrs. Corelly will have to retire after her operation. That leaves Chuck to run the store all by himself. It'll be hard on him.

   Well, in that case, why don't we make arrangements to _____ _____? They'd do the same thing for us.

4. I don't care what the others are saying. I'm on your side and I'll _____ _____.

   Thanks, dear, that's a great relief. That gives me confidence. I knew I could count on you.

5. I'm so glad you're home. Come right into the kitchen, I've got to talk to you. Something's come up.

   Oh dear, that doesn't sound good. Whatever it is, try to _____ _____. I have had an exceedingly hard day at the office, and the last thing I need is more trouble.

6. Wow, what a spread. I see you've set the table with candles and all, and look at that, even flowers. Say, what do you have in mind?

   Well, actually, it's a very carefully laid plan to _____, if you must know. Shall we start with champagne?

7. What are you so grouchy about all of a sudden, Ann? Aren't you having fun anymore?

   If you would stick to dancing with me, I wouldn't complain, but of course you've got to _____ all the other girls and then you start stepping all over my feet - that's not what I call having a good time.

8. You can lose 20 pounds in just one week on that diet, Madam, if you take advantage of our introductory offer now.

Oh? Well, I don't believe a word of your spiel, so why don't you pack up your super-duper slim display and be on your way. Do you really think I can't tell you're just trying to _____?

9. Little old Val in a barroom brawl? Surely that can't be true. You must have misheard.

   Everybody says that he could _____ but, believe me, once he's provoked, he can show quite a temper.

10. If you think it will help, we'll all walk into Mr. Ranken's office with you, just as long as you do the talking.

    Gee, that would be great. I'll be glad to present our problem to him. With you _____, he's much more likely to listen.

Idioms to choose from:

lend s.o. a helping hand
make eyes at s.o.
break it to s.o. gently
throw dust in s.o.'s eyes
treat s.o. with kid gloves
not harm a hair on s.o.'s head
sweep s.o. off their feet
go to bat for s.o.
give s.o. moral support
stick up for s.o.

UNIT 4 TEST YOURSELF

1. Susie eats more berries than she puts in her pail. Up to now I've ..., but if we expect to get enough to make jam, I'll have to make her whistle as she picks.
    a) kept her up to date
    b) cleared the air
    c) let it pass
    d) felt her out

2. I wondered why our cat came round the corner so fast. Then I realized that the neighbor's dog was
    a) putting a bug in her ear
    b) hard on her heels
    c) keeping her in check
    d) giving her the go-ahead

3. Mr. Brent has difficulty adding two and two. If he does the inventory, you'd better have someone ... if you expect an accurate tally.
    a) keep close tabs on him
    b) give him a broad hint
    c) put a bug in his ear
    d) go into a huddle with him

4. Harry talks about his great vacation in Tahiti all the time. He's gone and ..., but we can't afford a trip like that.
    a) put a bug in my husband's ear
    b) kept a tight rein on my husband
    c) risked his hide for us
    d) given it to us straight

5. On our team there are several players who'd like to ..., but the coach sees to it that everyone has a fair chance.
    a) keep hard on each other's heels
    b) dance to someone else's tune
    c) give the captain a broad hint
    d) rule the roost

6. Martin's a dreamer. He'll get involved in one impossible scheme after another if you don't
    a) let it pass
    b) keep him up to date
    c) let him get you down
    d) keep a tight rein on him

7. There must be a way to lick them. We'd better ... and see if we can't come up with it.
    a) risk our hide for them
    b) go into a huddle
    c) rule the roost
    d) give it to them straight

8. The city editor just called. She wants you to ... on the investigation so that she can print the latest facts.

   a) give her a broad hint
   b) clear the air
   c) add your 2 ¢ worth
   d) keep her up to date

9. Everything's ready for launching the campaign. We're just waiting for the Senator to

   a) give us the go-ahead
   b) be hard on our heels
   c) put a bug in our ear
   d) make us shape up

10. I'm tired of ... I'm going into business for *myself!*

    a) not letting it get me down.
    b) adding my 2 ¢ worth.
    c) dancing to someone else's tune.
    d) ruling the roost.

11. Fred would like to get on the boss's good side so that he'll get the promotion. But I'm ... by giving him so much work that he doesn't have time for fancy schemes.

    a) putting a bug in his ear
    b) keeping him in check
    c) keeping him up to date
    d) letting it pass

12. My mother kept inviting her younger male colleagues to dinner. She said she just wanted them to meet her daughter, but I ... She was just trying to marry me off.

    a) danced to her tune.
    b) ruled the roost.
    c) saw through her little game.
    d) gave it to her straight.

13. Every time somebody mentions food, Celia has to ..., even though she doesn't understand the first thing about cooking.

    a) put her 2 ¢ in
    b) go into a huddle
    c) give them the go-ahead
    d) let it pass

14. "Peter, I must talk to you. I can't go on with this thing between us. Let's sit down and

    a) go into a huddle."
    b) add our 2 ¢ worth."
    c) keep a tight rein on ourselves."
    d) clear the air."

15. So you didn't win in the lottery this week. ... You can try again next week.

    a) Give it to me straight from the shoulder!
    b) Don't let it get you down!
    c) Keep me in check!
    d) Give me the go-ahead!

16. The boss has noticed that Terry spends more time talking to friends on the phone than working. Unless you can ..., he's going to get fired.

    a) make him shape up
    b) keep close tabs on him
    c) risk your hide for him
    d) dance to his tune

17. Les is so unhappy about losing friend after friend that he's asking people to help him find the reason. Do you think that you can ... without hurting him too much?

    a) see through his little game
    b) feel him out
    c) give it to him straight from the shoulder
    d) keep a tight rein on him

18. Bruce wouldn't take no for an answer and kept calling Pam for a date. Finally she decided ... and showed up at his party with his best friend.

    a) to be hard on his heels
    b) to clear the air
    c) to put a bug in his ear
    d) to give him a broad hint

19. I sure would like to know whether Herbert has what it takes to handle this deal. Do you think you could ... at lunch and let me know this afternoon?

    a) see through his racket
    b) give him a broad hint
    c) make him shape up
    d) feel him out

* * * * *

UNIT 4 IDIOM ENTRIES AND USAGE
Interaction of Individuals (neutral)

4.1 *ein Auge zudrücken*

** let it pass **

used in a situation meriting reproach

But note: Her father had become an alcoholic, but she turned a blind eye to it. /ignored it/

4.2 *jdm auf den Fersen folgen*

** be hard on s.o.'s heels **

But note: stay on s.o.'s heels /maintain the pursuit/
follow on the heels of s.o./s.t. /sequentially/
I'm hard on my heels /wear my shoes down quickly/

4.3 *jdm auf die Finger sehen/schauen*

keep (close) tab(s) on s.o.

* Also: keep a close watch on s.o.
              sharp

4.4 *jdm einen Floh ins Ohr setzen*

put a bug in s.o.'s ear

* Also: put a bee in s.o.'s bonnet

4.5 *die erste Geige spielen*

rule the roost

OP: play second fiddle to s.o. (cf. 4.10)
But note: call the tune (1.19)

4.6 *jdn an der Kandare halten*

keep a tight rein on s.o.

OP: give free rein to s.o.
But note: take the reins (6.21)

4.7 *die Köpfe zusammenstecken*

go into a huddle

* Also: put one's heads together
usu. non-conspiratorial
See also: mit jdm unter einer Decke stecken (5.4)

4.8 *jdn auf dem laufenden halten*

keep s.o. up to date

* Also: keep s.o. posted
But note: keep s.o. on the run /keep s.o. moving or retreating/

4.9 *(jdm) grünes Licht geben*

give (s.o.) the go-ahead

4.10 *nach jds Pfeife/Geige tanzen*

dance to s.o. (else)'s tune

* Also: play second fiddle to s.o.
OP: call the tune (1.19)
But note: dance to another tune /act differently/

4.11 *jdn in Schach halten*

keep s.o. in check
hold

But note: keep a check on s.o. /observe/

4.12   jdm auf die Schliche kommen

   ** see through s.o.'s racket **
                    (little) game **

   * Also: be up to s.o.'s tricks
                 get on the track of s.t./s.o.
   NEG also: fail to see through s.o.'s racket
   Note also: They didn't see through his racket /were duped/

4.13   seinen Senf dazugeben

   ** add one's two cents (worth) **

   ** put in one's two cents (worth) **

4.14   reinen Tisch machen

   ** clear the air **

   Note also: They had a little talk and that cleared the air between them.
                 make a clean breast of s.t. /confess/

4.15   sich nicht unterkriegen lassen

   ** not let s.o./s.t. get one down **

   * Also: never say die!
   See also: die Ohren steif halten (1.17)

4.16   jdn auf Vordermann bringen

   ** make s.o. shape up **

4.17   jdm reinen Wein einschenken

   ** give it to s.o. straight (from the shoulder) **

   See also: kein Blatt vor den Mund nehmen (1.1)

4.18   jdm einen Wink mit dem Zaunpfahl geben

   ** give s.o. a broad hint **

   But note: give someone a gentle hint (3.3)

4.19   jdm auf den Zahn fühlen

   ** feel s.o. out ** /try to find out what s.o. thinks or can do/

   * Also: get a reading on s.o.
                 try s.o.'s mettle /endurance, courage/
   But note: give s.o. the once-over /quick examination/
   Note also: sound s.o. out /try to find out what s.o. thinks/
   See also: bei jdm auf den Busch klopfen (7.5)

* * * * * * *

4.20   jdn um den kleinen Finger wickeln

   ** wrap s.o. around one's (little) finger **

4.21 (jdm) sein Herz ausschütten
     ** pour one's heart out (to s.o.) **

4.22 die Karten (offen) auf den Tisch legen
     ** lay one's cards on the table **

4.23 die Katze aus dem Sack lassen
     ** let the cat out of the bag **

* * * * *

UNIT 4 RECOGNITION

1. keep tabs on someone
2. keep a tight rein on someone
3. let it pass
4. see through someone's racket

   a) make a record of
   b) choose to overlook something
   c) watch someone closely
   d) not be duped by a scheme
   e) cause to happen
   f) restrain someone's actions

5. go into a huddle
6. put a bug in someone's ear
7. keep someone up to date
8. add one's two cents worth

   a) provide with fashionable clothes
   b) provide with current information
   c) make an unreasonable suggestion
   d) contribute a little money to a good cause
   e) express an opinion unasked
   f) plan something together

9. give (someone) the go-ahead
10. make someone shape up
11. rule the roost
12. be hard on someone's heels

   a) wear out someone's shoes
   b) be in charge
   c) be in close pursuit
   d) cause someone to mend his ways
   e) authorize someone's plans
   f) put someone on a diet

13. clear the air
    a) open the window
    b) settle a difference
    c) eliminate smog
    d) have a quarrel

14. not let someone get you down
    a) stay in a key position
    b) take preventive medicine
    c) retain a positive attitude
    d) avoid pitfalls

15. dance to someone (else)'s tune
    a) copy someone
    b) learn a new step
    c) do what someone else wants
    d) work in a team

16. give it to someone straight
    a) provide someone with new data
    b) hand someone a drink with no ice
    c) tell the unadulterated truth regardless
    d) give it to someone right away

17. give someone a broad hint
    a) provide with an obvious cue
    b) tell someone all the details
    c) inform on someone
    d) provide with excess information

18. feel someone out
    a) make someone leave
    b) try to find out what someone thinks or can do
    c) ask for specific information
    d) audition someone

19. hold (someone) in check
    a) keep in prison
    b) keep an eye on
    c) exercise control over
    d) be a creditor to

* * * * *

UNIT 4 STORY COMPLETION

All right, men, the reason I had you fall in next to the barracks is that your performance has not been satisfactory so far. For one, we need to do something about the fact that you're moving too slow, but since I have more important things to say to you, I'll _____ _____ _____ (skip it) for now. For instance, there is dirt on your boots, DIRT! You better shape up or your first sergeant will be _____ _____ _____ _____ (hounding you) about your appearance. Men, I'll _____ _____ _____ _____ _____ (watch every step of) every one of you from now on. If you think I'm kidding, like Daddy is just _____ _____ _____ _____ _____ _____ (giving you a wild notion), you've got another guess coming. Heed my words, or the consequences for you will be terrible. Let this be a word to the wise.

Next item. It has come to my attention that you barracks leaders order the other soldiers around as if you're the ones who ___ ___ ___ (are in command). This will cease at once. There is enough leadership already to ___ ___ ___ ___ ___ (narrowly constrain) every darned soldier in the company. What is that commotion there in the fourth column? Stand at attention, you zeros! If I wanted you to ___ ___ ___ ___ (talk privately) back there, I'd tell you so. If you move as much as an eyelash you'll be recruits until hell freezes over.

Now, where was I? Ah yes, your request for me to ___ ___ ___ ___ ___ (provide current information) on the availability of weekend passes. Passes are now authorized by the captain, and he has ___ ___ ___ ___ - ___ (allows me) to issue a pass to those soldiers who stand tall during inspection. So, let me make myself perfectly clear: Either you ___ ___ ___ ___ (do exactly as I say) starting right now, or you can kiss your weekend pass good-by, you wash-outs. And don't you get into trouble between now and then. To help ___ ___ ___ ___ (maintain order among you), there will be a G.I. party to clean up the barracks, if necessary until reveille. And that place better sparkle when I come to inspect it. Don't even try to just hide the dirt, I'll ___ ___ ___ ___ ___ (be alert to your deceptions) all right, you hear me? What are you mumbling there, Brubaker, ha? Ha? No need for you to ___ ___ ___ ___ ___ ___ (add your opinion) either, you smart-alec. You come to full attention instantly or I'll show you who's boss around here.

Well, I feel better now after this little friendly talk I had to give you; that should ___ ___ ___ (re-establish friendly relations) between us. You do your job right, and nobody will bother you. So get smart, men, and don't ___ the Service ___ ___ ___ (feel bad about). Once the Army ___ ___ ___ ___ (gets you to behave appropriately), you'll be standing tall and will be a credit to the Service. All right, I've ___ ___ ___ ___ ___ ___ ___ ___ (told you candidly). Now that you troops have been ___ ___ ___ ___ (told indirectly but unmistakeably), you know where you stand, so don't any of you come crying on my shoulder later or clutter up my orderly room trying to ___ ___ ___ (glean information) as to how much you can put over on me. It'll be tough on you, I promise you that. All right, men, fall out and get those barracks shining like your mother never could. You can, you zeros, and you will. Fall out!

UNIT 4 *SITUATION FIT*

1. "I think it's wonderful that you hired William when nobody else would give him a chance because he's been in jail."

   "Well, I don't believe in condemning someone forever just because he's made one mistake. Nevertheless, I'd appreciate it if you'd _____ ____ for the first few weeks and let me know how he's working out."

2. "This building is a mess. Is it always like this?"

   "No, just since our old janitor's been in the hospital. We do have someone taking his place, but he doesn't appear to be very conscientious."

   "You should complain about that man to your tenants' association. They ought to _____ or find someone else."

3. "Our new business manager thinks he's a real hot-shot and is trying to tyrannize the rest of the staff into submission."

   "I don't think we really need to worry. The president's not likely to let anyone else_____ and will set him straight on that as soon as she gets wind of it."

4. "What is that incredible stack of papers on your desk?"

   "Don't ask. I'm going through all the newspapers to try to get a reading on public opinion. The boss has asked me to_____ about people's reactions to the shopping center we proposed at the last city council meeting."

5. "I honestly don't know what to do about Mrs. James. Her work is not what it used to be. She's becoming more and more unreliable."

   "If I were you, I'd_____ for the moment. She's going through a difficult phase right now, with her husband in the hospital and quite a financial burden to cope with. I'm sure everything will get back to normal again once her husband goes back to work."

6. "Well, if you ask me, what this town needs is a new mayor."

"Well, I didn't ask you, and I can do without having you _____ _____. You simply don't understand the problems we're facing. What we need is more money, not a new face in town hall."

7. "Do you have any idea of what's going on at the budget committee meeting today?"

"Not really, but apparently something big is up. Steve said he's heard a lot of whispering about money and debts. I hope the bosses aren't _____ _____ just to figure out how to break some bad news to us in the least painful way."

8. "What's the matter with you?"

"Nothing's the matter with *me*. It's our daughter who's driving me up the wall. Ever since Mary_____ about going to the Halloween dance, she's been trying out the most ridiculous costume ideas -- and of course every one of them would require me to do most of the sewing."

9. "We ought to talk about Richard. He seems to be running around with a pretty wild crowd."

"Yeah. I've been thinking about that, too. I suppose we'd better_____ _____ and see to it that he spends more time with the family and on his homework."

10. "Monica just mentioned that she's almost 30. That reminded me that her birthday is next week."

"You're right. I'd forgotten, too. I guess that was her way to_____ _____. Let's be grateful for it. I'd never have forgiven myself for having missed the occasion."

11. "What do you suggest as a plan of action?"

"We can't commit ourselves yet. It seems to me that the most important thing is to figure out a way to_____ our competitors _____until our own financing has come through and we can jump on that contract ourselves."

43

12. "Why so excited?"

   "I can't wait for class to be over so I can head downtown to the used car lot. Dad's finally _____ for a car of my own."

13. "Do you think we'll be able to gain enough support between now and election day to be considered serious contenders?"

   "Definitely. We're _____ of our opponents now and it won't take much to overtake them."

14. "Have you heard from Aunt Mildred lately?"

   "No, and I know why. Ever since the difficulties we had in settling grandfather's estate, there seems to be a cloud over our relationship. But I'm ready to write to her now. It really is time to _____ and get back on a friendly footing again."

15. "Aren't you going to invite Walter to your party?"

   "No. He's ignored me for weeks. And now that he's heard I'm giving a party, he's suddenly very friendly again. But I _____. He's not interested in me, all he wants is an invitation."

16. "You and Steve seem more like strangers lately than old friends. Has something come between you?"

   "I'm afraid we're not on the same wavelength anymore. Instead of standing on his own two feet, he _____ his new girlfriend's _____ all the time, and I can't stand to watch that."

17. "I don't know what we're going to do. The kids have said 'Oh, we don't want to go there' about every place we've suggested for our family vacation."

   "Oh, _____. Kids always have to be different. Besides, I suspect what is really the matter is that they want to go off on their own with their friends."

18. "Do you think we can hire Nancy for this rather delicate job?"

"I think so, but I've asked our sales manager to _____ just to make sure I'm not letting her big blue eyes influence my judgement."

19. "I wish I could figure out some way to make Mark understand without hurting his feelings that his unending visits are quite a burden."

"I don't think that's possible. I tried repeatedly, but he never took the hint. You'll just have to _____ if you expect him to get the message."

Idioms to choose from:

let it pass
be hard on s.o.'s heels
keep (close) tab(s) on s.o.
put a bug in s.o.'s ear
rule the roost
keep a tight rein on s.o.
go into a huddle
keep s.o. up to date
give s.o. the go-ahead
dance to s.o. (else's) tune
keep s.o. in check
see through s.o.'s little game
add one's two cents worth
clear the air
not let s.o./s.t. get one down
make s.o. shape up
give it to s.o. straight
give s.o. a broad hint
feel s.o. out

UNIT 5 TEST YOURSELF

1. Jack wanted to take Carol out on a date tonight, but his dad wouldn't let him have the car keys. He really

    a) put his foot in it
    b) put a spoke in Jack's wheel
    c) threw a scare into Jack
    d) had Jack's head

2. Joe isn't diplomatic enough. I'd say don't promote him to office supervisor. It will only

    a) throw a scare into everybody
    b) be music to his ears
    c) breed bad blood
    d) pull the wool over everybody's eyes

3. When John pulled out of the driveway so fast and acted as if he was going to run over me, he really

    a) threw a scare into me
    b) put his foot in it
    c) beat me to a pulp
    d) drew a bead on me

4. First he escapes from prison in broad daylight. Then his guards disappear. I bet they were all

    a) playing into each other's hand
    b) taking him in
    c) taken in by him
    d) in cahoots with each other

5. We tried to catch Maxine with her hand in the till. And sure enough, she

    a) walked right into our trap
    b) lured us into a trap
    c) played into our hands
    d) slipped through our fingers

6. The police used a decoy to finally

    a) put a spoke in his wheel
    b) pay him back in kind
    c) lure him into a trap
    d) take him in

7. Harry's wife died 3 years ago. So when someone asked him at a party last week how she was, he really

    a) paid him back in kind
    b) put his foot in it
    c) took him in
    d) bred bad blood

8. When my prediction actually came true two days later, it

   a) put my foot in it
   b) pulled the wool over my eyes
   c) was music to my ears
   d) took me in completely

9. No wonder they got divorced. They were constantly

   a) in each other's hair
   b) drawing a bead on each other
   c) pulling the wool over each other's eyes
   d) beating each other to a pulp

10. There would have been a serious injury if the police hadn't moved in quickly. They were about to

    a) grind each other to a pulp
    b) be taken in by them
    c) breed bad blood
    d) get in each other's hair

11. When the boss let me handle the Miller contract, I knew he was

    a) in cahoots with me
    b) walking into my trap
    c) playing right into my hand
    d) drawing a bead on me

12. If the boss finds out that we dropped the crate with the antique vase, he'll

    a) be in cahoots with us
    b) have our heads
    c) slip through our fingers
    d) pay us back in kind

13. It soon became obvious that if Henry continued to throw spitballs at his classmates, the teacher would

    a) draw a bead on him
    b) lure him into a trap
    c) be taken in by him
    d) breed bad blood

14. It wasn't until after the check bounced that Barb realized the used car lot had

    a) walked into her trap
    b) put a spoke into her wheel
    c) taken her in
    d) played into her hand

15. By changing directions on us five times, that clever little crook finally fooled us and

    a) put a spoke in our wheel
    b) had our heads
    c) walked into our trap
    d) slipped through our fingers

16. Look, Jane, when I left the house I had a twenty on me. Now I come back with a newspaper and some cigarettes and do you see what I have left? Thirteen dollars. I swear I was

    a) lured into a trap by that clerk
    b) taken in by that clerk
    c) beaten to a pulp
    d) in cahoots with that clerk

17. If we tell Dad that we're on our way to class and then skip school instead, that would be

    a) music to his ears
    b) throwing a scare into him
    c) pulling the wool over his eyes
    d) slipping through his fingers

18. If your supervisor continues to treat you like dirt, you'll have to

    a) pay him back in kind
    b) get into each other's hair
    c) have his head
    d) slip through his fingers

                       * * * * *

UNIT 5 IDIOM ENTRIES AND USAGE
Interaction of Individuals (negative)

5.1 *jdm das/ein Bein stellen*

   ** put a spoke in s.o.'s wheel **

   But note: trip s.o. up = trap s.o. into making a mistake

5.2 *böses Blut erregen*

   ** breed bad blood **
   ** cause

5.3 *jdn ins Bockshorn jagen*

   ** throw a scare into s.o. ** /not necessarily intentional/

5.4 *mit jdm unter einer Decke stecken*

   ** be in cahoots with s.o. **
         league

   usu. conspiratorial
   See also: die Köpfe zusammenstecken (4.7)

5.5 *jdm in die Falle gehen / jdm ins Netz gehen*

   ** walk into s.o.'s trap **

   REV: lure s.o. into a trap (5.6)
   See also: jdm auf den Leim gehen (5.16)

5.6 *jdn in die Falle locken*

** lure s.o. into a trap **

REV: walk into s.o.'s trap (5.5)
* Also: take s.o. for a ride
See also: jdn hinters Licht führen (5.17)

5.7 *ins Fettnäpfchen treten*

** put one's foot in it **

* Also: commit a faux-pas
step in it
drop a brick

5.8 *für jdn ein gefundenes Fressen sein*

** be music to s.o.'s ears ** /good tidings/

* Also: be grist to s.o.'s mill /easy to capitalize on/

5.9 *sich in den Haaren liegen*

** get in each other's hair **
** be

But note: get in s.o.'s hair (non-reciprocally) = bother s.o.

5.10 *aus jdm Hackfleisch machen*

** beat s.o. to a pulp **
** grind
** make mincemeat out of s.o. **

usu. said as a threat

5.11 *jdm eine Karte in die Hand spielen*

** play (right) into s.o.'s hand **

5.12 *jds Kopf rollen lassen*

** have s.o.'s head **

* Also: give s.o. the sack
ax
Note also: Heads will roll. /prediction/

5.13 *jdn aufs Korn nehmen*

** draw a bead on s.o. **

* Also: gun for s.o.
But note: zero in on s.t. /give one's full attention to it/

5.14 *jdn aufs Kreuz legen*

** take s.o. in **

REV: be taken in by s.o. (5.16)
But note: pin s.o. down /get s.o. to commit himself to a position/
take s.o. in /also = shelter s.o./

5.15   *jdm durch die Lappen gehen*

   ** slip through s.o.'s fingers **

5.16   *jdm auf den Leim gehen*

   ** be taken in by s.o. **

   REV: take s.o. in (5.14)
   See also: jdm in die Falle gehen (5.5)

5.17   *jdn hinters Licht führen*

   ** pull the wool over s.o.'s eyes **

   * Also: lead s.o. up the garden path
   See also: jdn in die Falle locken (5.6)
               jdn blauen Dunst vormachen (3.4)

5.18   *jdm mit gleicher Münze heimzahlen*

   ** pay s.o. back in kind **

   * Also: give (s.o.) tit for tat
               give as good as one gets
               give s.o. a taste of his/her own medicine

* * * * * * *

5.19   *jdm den Hals brechen*

   ** break s.o.'s neck **

5.20   *jdm einen Maulkorb umhängen*

   ** put a muzzle on s.o. **

5.21   *(jdm) die Schau stehlen*

   ** steal the show (from s.o.) **

* * * * *

UNIT 5   RECOGNITION

1. put a spoke in s.o.'s wheel
   a) foil s.o.'s plans
   b) cause s.o. to have an accident
   c) repair s.t. for s.o.
   d) disturb s.o.

2. breed bad blood
   a) incite others to riot
   b) inherit disease
   c) set off a family feud
   d) aggravate a situation

3. throw a scare into s.o.
   a) give s.o. a fright
   b) tell s.o. a ghost story
   c) attempt to safeguard one's property
   d) threaten retaliation

4. walk into s.o.'s trap
   a) venture into danger
   b) be silenced by s.o.
   c) get caught in s.o.'s web
   d) fall into a hole

5. put one's foot in it
   a) have an accident
   b) step on s.o.'s foot
   c) make a social error
   d) reveal startling news

6. slip through s.o.'s fingers
   a) be difficult to pin down
   b) get away
   c) be ruined
   d) be lost through carelessness

7. be taken in by s.o.
   a) get cheated
   b) get admitted
   c) be led through
   d) lose a bet

8. pull the wool over s.o.'s eyes
   a) deceive s.o.
   b) play hide and seek with s.o.
   c) blindfold s.o.
   d) act as decoy

9. be music to s.o.'s ears
   a) sound pleasant
   b) be listened to attentively
   c) provide a soothing effect
   d) what one is delighted to hear

10. grind s.o. to a pulp
    a) destroy s.o.'s career
    b) train s.o. to write popular fiction
    c) beat s.o. up
    d) criticize scathingly

11. lure s.o. into a trap _____
12. have s.o.'s head _____
13. take s.o. in _____
14. draw a bead on s.o. _____

   a) point the finger at s.o.
   b) mislead s.o. to their disadvantage
   c) go after someone
   d) execute s.o.
   e) report s.o. to the police
   f) fire s.o.
   g) fool s.o.

15. be in cahoots with s.o. _____
16. play (right) into s.o.'s hand _____
17. get in each other's hair _____
18. pay s.o. back in kind _____

a) hold a grudge against
b) repay a favor
c) conspire with
d) play on the same team
e) argue with one another
f) inadvertently facilitate s.o.'s plans
g) be in each other's way
h) give as one gets

* * * * *

UNIT 5 STORY COMPLETION

Gentlemen, I'd like to call the meeting to order. I don't need to tell you that we have a real problem situation on our hands. Our competitors are hell-bent on moving in on our product line; market-wise, they are trying to _____ _____ _____ _____ _____ _____ *(obstruct our plans),* and we need to develop some strategy to maintain our lead. I'm for a really aggressive sales campaign in their territories, even if that _____ _____ _____ *(aggravates relations)* for a while. If we move fast, we'll _____ _____ _____ _____ _____ *(frighten them)* right from the start, and soon our White Gold Tuna will outsell theirs two-to-one. We've done it before, and we can do it again. And, Gentlemen, we will have to hit all of them at the same time and cover the entire area with our products. The fact that they all moved in on us at the same time shows that these companies have planned a joint campaign and _____ _____ _____ _____ _____ _____ *(are conspiring),* but we're onto their scheme now, and we won't _____ _____ _____ _____ *(be caught by them)* by trying to keep them out of our area. Instead, we'll flood their own outlet area with White Gold. Now here is my plan: As soon as their managements notice that we're not fighting them on our home ground as expected but are heavily advertising in their home territories instead and flooding the market with our own specials, they'll have to shift their attention back home to save what they can. But they are spread thin over too wide a territory, and so we'll actually be _____ _____ _____ _____ _____ *(drawing them into calamity).* As soon as they become unsure of what's happening, we move back into our own area and re-establish our superiority there. All this is absolutely confidential, of course, so don't anybody _____ _____ _____ _____ _____ *(blunder)* by making unguarded statements which could reveal our strategy. That, of course, would _____ _____ _____ _____ _____ *(be welcome news to them),* so watch it. I want all of you to work together for the good of the company. It is imperative that you don't interfere with your fellow sales representatives or _____ _____ _____ _____ _____ *(interfere with each other)* for

the sake of a quick profit. I'll _____ _____ _____ _____ _any_ _of_ _____
(treat you roughly) who go against my orders. Let me explain why: Anyone who
goes his own way in the next critical months is in effect _____ _____ _____
_____ _____ *(aiding and abetting)* the competition, and I'll _____ _____
_____ *(fire him)*. We've got to stick together as long as the compeltion is trying
to _____ _____ _____ _____ _____ *(focus on us threateningly)*. The
strategy I have outlined to you is bound to _____ _____ _____ *(deceive them)*
and will therefore give us the advantage in the tuna business for years. If we
don't succeed here and now, it will mean a loss in earnings to you, so don't let
any opportunity _____ _____ _____ _____ *(escape inadvertently)* if you
can help it. If the competition tries to hire you away from us, don't _____ _____
_____ _____ _____ *(let them deceive you)* and their promise of high earnings.
It would only be a cheap attempt to _____ _____ _____ _____ _____ _____
(fool you)! Later on, they would drop you cold. So, to sum up, Gentlemen, our
competitors have declared a price war on us and we are going to meet the challenge.
Let's _____ _____ _____ _____ _____ *(give as we get)*!

* * * * *

UNIT 5 SITUATION FIT

1. No secrets, I was just talking to the boys. Why do you ask?

    Oh, no reason. By the way, I don't believe you. I'm sure you're _____
    _____ about something, like another fishing trip, but it won't
    take me long to find out, and I absolutely refuse to be bored stiff sitting by
    another lake.

2. Did you say this toaster you bought at the flea market was brand new? It's got crumbs in the bottom.

    Yes, I noticed that on the way home. But the salesman's manner was so
    pleasant and reassuring that he _____ completely.

3. What if we install time clocks for our employees in an attempt to curb absenteeism?

    Hold on a minute, that may be too restrictive and could _____
    _____ in the end. How about trying a circular for the time being? Perhaps
    it will have the desired effect and won't upset folks.

4. That guy makes me furious. He said he had to study all weekend, and then I saw him go into the pizza parlor with another girl. I'll have to teach him a lesson, but how?

   Just _____ and start dating others yourself. But be sure he sees you on a date, too!

5. Did you buy that new stove?

   No, the clerk tried to tell me they're no longer being manufactured and wanted to sell me a more expensive one. But he was just trying to _____, because I know for a fact that the model I want is still in production.

6. Oh, your mother is coming for the entire weekend again? How about telling her we're painting and she is welcome to help us?

   Well, that ought to _____ all right; she hates a lot of commotion. But what about the next time she comes and sees that we didn't paint after all?

7. Either you get out of my way right now or you're going to be real sorry, Mac. So move!

   Look, you, if you take another step I'll _____, you hear? I've wanted to get my hands on you for a long time, so you just try it.

8. I couldn't think of a way to get rid of him except to tell him I would only go out with him if he took a shower beforehand.

   Anybody else would think you had really _____ and be offended, but you never know with him.

9. But it's supposed to be for a good cause. Are you sure we shouldn't help that poor fellow? The subscription is only 12 dollars.

   Don't _____ yet another door-to-door salesman, for crying out loud. Can't you tell they all give you the same sob story?

10. I've told Jim that he has to clean up the backyard this weekend, and that I want to see the car washed and waxed before Monday. Do you think I'm too tough on him?

   Well, that will certainly _____, won't it? He's usually off with his friends from morning till night.

11. It was John who dropped that crate off the truck, not me, so will you get off my back?

   All right, where did he go? He's ruined 500 dollars worth of merchandise, and it's not the first time either. This time I'll _____.

12. Did you see him come out?

   No, not here, at least. I hate to tell you -- somehow he's managed to _____ _____, but we're bound to catch up with him eventually.

13. That must be our young ones coming home, judging from the shouting and screaming.

   Yes, that's right. The way they _____ all the time, you'd never guess they're sisters. I bet they've been after the same boy again.

14. Why not sneak out the back way? Tim will never catch you that way.

   Yes, but if he's smart, he'll have one of his buddies posted out there, and I may be _____, because then he actually could accuse me of being a coward.

15. Let's let the chairman make that motion. We can tie up the voting for any length of time if we keep the discussion going.

   Yes, and that way he will actually _____ without meaning to, and we won't even be identified with introducing the issue.

16. You're sure in trouble in that geography class. What does Mr. Green have against you that he always calls on you when nobody else knows the answer?

   I don't know, but he's _____ every opportunity he gets. I think he's found out how bored I am in his class.

17. Would you believe my luck? I tried to introduce the topic of square-dancing all along, and then she brought it up herself.

    That must have _____. So we can expect you at the barn dance this Sunday, right?

18. Look, why don't you call at his house and say he's urgently wanted down at the drugstore, and then you catch him before he can go in?

    If he falls for it. It's not so easy to _____ that way, especially when he's expecting it. Think again.

Idioms to choose from:

put a spoke in s.o.'s wheel
breed bad blood
throw a scare into s.o.
be in cahoots with s.o.
walk into s.o.'s trap
lure s.o. into a trap
put one's foot in it
be music to one's ears
be in each other's hair
beat s.o. to a pulp
play into s.o.'s hand
have s.o.'s head
draw a bead on s.o.
take s.o. in
slip through s.o.'s fingers
be taken in by s.o.
pull the wool over s.o.'s eyes
pay s.o. back in kind

UNIT 6   TEST YOURSELF

1. I have the feeling that Senator White is so set on getting this bill through Congress that he would
    a) take up arms for it
    b) pull the chestnuts out of the fire
    c) kill two birds with one stone
    d) paint the town red

2. Since Ed and Mary bought the house privately, they picked it up for less than market value. Ed was not exaggerating when he said they
    a) saved for a rainy day
    b) got it for a song
    c) made both ends meet
    d) cashed in on it

3. With inflation eating into their income, many people today really have serious problems
    a) striking while the iron is hot
    b) standing their ground
    c) making both ends meet
    d) putting their shoulder to the wheel

4. While you're downtown shopping, could you pick up the laundry? That way you could
    a) make both ends meet
    b) pull the chestnuts out of the fire
    c) hit the nail on the head
    d) kill two birds with one stone

5. While you're talking to the boss about the Thompson contract you just landed for the company, don't pass up the opportunity to ask for a raise. Remember, you've got to
    a) take up arms for it
    b) bring all your guns to bear on him
    c) strike while the iron is hot
    d) stand your ground

6. The committee has been instructed to slash expenditures and will be reluctant to take any action, so the only way to get your proposal through is to
    a) bring all your guns to bear on them
    b) have a firm grip on them
    c) be securely in the driver's seat
    d) carry off the palm

7. The effective way the governor always supports his argument with statistics shows that he
    a) carries off the palm
    b) takes the reins
    c) starts the ball rolling
    d) has a firm grip on the facts

8. Joe's repeated attempts to get a loan from his father indicate to me that he will ... to start his own business.

    a) take the bull by the horns
    b) have the money handed to him on a silver platter
    c) get the ball rolling
    d) move heaven and earth

9. If your mother-in-law wants you to iron your husband's underwear, just don't give in this time. For once, you must

    a) stand your ground!
    b) move heaven and earth!
    c) strike while the iron is hot!
    d) take up arms for your husband!

10. You have no idea how reassuring it is to have the house paid off. For once, we'll be able to

    a) get something for a song
    b) be securely in the driver's seat
    c) save something for a rainy day
    d) pull the chestnuts out of the fire

11. When Max's rental car broke down halfway to Florida, he not only talked the agency into giving him a more luxurious replacement, he got two extra days of unlimited mileage free. Did he

    a) cash in on that deal!
    b) carry off the palm!
    c) get things handed to him on a silver platter!
    d) hit the bull's-eye!

12. For months they didn't inform me that the negotiations weren't going well. Now that there is a stalemate, I'm supposed to

    a) kill two birds with one stone
    b) have a firm grip on the matter
    c) paint the town red
    d) pull the chestnuts out of the fire

13. Celebrations were in order after the last exam, and so they decided to

    a) get something for a song
    b) bring all their guns to bear on it
    c) paint the town red
    d) take the bull by the horns

14. Since John is the only candidate, there isn't the slightest doubt who will

    a) carry off the palm
    b) take the reins
    c) cash in on the election
    d) put his shoulder to the wheel

15. Wilga offered to contribute three attractive prizes for the contest we are holding. I'm confident that will

    a) put our shoulder to the wheel
    b) start the ball rolling
    c) move heaven and earth
    d) hit the bull's-eye

16. The fact that the dictator is unworried about leaving the capital for a long vacation shows you he's
    a) taking up arms for the country
    b) securely in the driver's seat
    c) taking the reins of the country
    d) taking the bull by the horns

17. Unless we oppose Cathy's nomination for the executive presidency, we will be the first ones to blame for
    a) having handed her the company on a silver platter
    b) pulling the chestnuts out of the fire
    c) cashing in on the company
    d) bringing all our guns to bear on the matter

18. Heather hadn't expected everyone to agree with her so readily, but she was very glad to note that her remarks had
    a) made both ends meet
    b) killed two birds with one stone
    c) hit the bull's-eye
    d) a firm grip on the audience

19. Frank gave up waiting for the unemployment office to find him a job. By placing an ad in all the papers and calling a number of companies, he
    a) had a firm grip on the situation
    b) took the bull by the horns
    c) struck while the iron was hot
    d) stood his ground

20. Ever since he flunked math, that boy has really
    a) been securely in the driver's seat
    b) started the ball rolling
    c) put his shoulder to the wheel
    d) moved heaven and earth

21. Paul has been in the business for many years; now that his father has retired and turned over the plant to him, Paul should have no trouble in
    a) taking the reins
    b) getting a tighter rein on the business
    c) getting the business for a song
    d) saving something for a rainy day

* * * * *

UNIT 6   *IDIOM ENTRIES AND USAGE*
          Individual and World (positive)

6.1   *für etwas auf die Barrikaden gehen/steigen*

   ** take up arms for s.t. **

   But note: go to bat for *someone* (3.8)

6.2   *etwas für ein Butterbrot bekommen*

   ** get s.t. for a song **

6.3 *sich nach der Decke strecken*
   ** make (both) ends meets **
   NEG and QUES without "both"
   But note: reach for the sky /aim high/

6.4 *zwei Fliegen mit einer Klappe schlagen*
   ** kill two birds with one stone **

6.5 *die Gelegenheit beim Schopf packen*
   ** strike while the iron is hot **
   But note: take the bull by the horns (6.19)

6.6 *ein grobes/schweres Geschütz auffahren*
   ** bring all one's guns to bear on s.t./s.o. **
   * Also: bring up the big guns

6.7 *etwas fest in der Hand haben*
   ** have a firm grip on s.t. **
   * Also: have s.t. well under control
                 in hand
   OP: lose one's grip on s.t.
   But note: have s.t. on hand /available/
              have s.t. handy /within easy reach/

6.8 *alle Hebel in Bewegung setzen*
   ** move heaven and earth **
   But note: leave no stone unturned /be thorough/

6.9 *sich auf die Hinterbeine stellen*
   ** stand one's ground **
   * Also: dig one's heels in

6.10 *etwas auf die hohe Kante legen*
   ** save (s.t.) for a rainy day **

6.11 *aus etwas Kapital schlagen*
   ** cash in on s.t. **
   But note: I sent her the check and she cashed it. We needed money and cashed in our savings certificates.

6.12 *die Karre aus dem Dreck ziehen*
   ** pull the chestnuts out of the fire (for s.o.) **

6.13 *auf die Pauke hauen*
   ** paint the town (red) **
   But note: beat the drum for s.o./s.t. /advertise/

6.14 *das Rennen machen*

    ** carry off the palm **
    ** bear

    * Also: carry the day

6.15 *etwas ins Rollen bringen*

    ** start the ball rolling **
    ** get

    But note: get a move on /hurry up/

6.16 *(fest/sicher) im Sattel sitzen*

    ** be (securely) in the driver's seat **

    See also: alle Fäden in der Hand halten (1.2)

6.17 *jdm fällt etwas in den Schoß*

    ** have s.t. handed to one on a silver platter **
    ** get

    * Also: s.t. falls right into one's lap

6.18 *ins Schwarze treffen*

    ** hit the bull's-eye **
           target **
           mark **

    * Also: be right on target
                 hit the nail on the head
    But note: make one's mark /make a name for oneself/

6.19 *den Stier bei den Hörnern packen*

    ** take the bull by the horns **
    ** grab

    But note: strike while the iron is hot /take advantage of an opportunity, cf. 6.5/

6.20 *sich (tüchtig) ins Zeug legen*

    ** put one's shoulder to the wheel **

    * Also: put one's back to it

6.21 *die Zügel / das Ruder in die Hand nehmen*

    ** take the reins **
             wheel **
             helm **

    But note: get a tighter rein on s.t./s.o.
                 keep a tight rein on s.o. (4.6)

* * * * * * *

6.22 *den Fuß in der Tür haben*

    ** have one's foot in the door **

6.23 den Nagel auf den Kopf treffen
      ** hit the nail on the head **

6.24 die Kastanien aus dem Feuer holen
      ** pull the chestnuts out of the fire (cf. 6.12) **

* * * * *

UNIT 6 RECOGNITION

1. take up arms for s.t.   _____
2. kill two birds with one stone   _____
3. bring all one's guns to bear on _____
4. hit the bull's-eye   _____

   a) score a fencing hit
   b) achieve more than one thing at a time
   c) support a cause
   d) call for reinforcements
   e) do or say s.t. apropos
   f) get drafted
   g) act as a counterspy
   h) use maximal effort to persuade

5. stand one's ground   _____
6. take the bull by the horns   _____
7. put one's shoulder to the
    wheel   _____
8. take the helm   _____

   a) work in dangerous circumstances
   b) not give up under adversity
   c) try to prevent damage
   d) carry a heavy burden
   e) tackle a difficult problem courageously
   f) purchase property
   g) put much effort into s.t.
   h) move into control

9. get s.t. for a song   _____
10. save for a rainy day   _____
11. cash in on s.t.   _____
12. get s.t. handed to one on a
    silver platter   _____

   a) take timely advantage of something
   b) earn a lot of money
   c) put aside for emergencies
   d) pay very little for s.t.
   e) get s.t. without effort
   f) plan to buy a house
   g) put s.t. off for a while

13. pull the chestnuts out of the fire
    a) get dinner ready
    b) be responsible for meals at camp
    c) make amends
    d) help s.o. out of a predicament

14. paint the town red
    a) celebrate something
    b) decorate in garish colors
    c) put your mark on s.t.
    d) eradicate a general ill

15. carry off the palm
    a) get rid of junk
    b) end up the winner
    c) act like the big boss
    d) gossip about s.o.

16. start the ball rolling
    a) take the first turn
    b) be referee at the lottery drawing
    c) initiate an activity or action
    d) overcome initial inertia

17. be securely in the driver's seat
    a) authorize an action
    b) behave consistently
    c) be in command of the situation
    d) take sufficient precautions

18. make (both) ends meet
    a) bring feuding parties back together
    b) finish an undertaking
    c) cope according to the situation
    d) not have enough money

19. strike while the iron is hot
    a) get up early
    b) act while you still can
    c) take immediate advantage of an opportunity
    d) outsmart an opponent

20. have a firm grip on s.t.
    a) have a stranglehold on s.t.
    b) have s.t. well under control
    c) understand s.t. completely
    d) exercise financial control over

21. move heaven and earth
    a) pray and beg for s.t.
    b) be thorough about doing s.t.
    c) exploit all means to reach a goal
    d) cause fundamental changes

* * * * *

UNIT 6 STORY COMPLETION

Son: "Maybe you haven't been paying attention to this, Dad, but Mom has decided to join a cause. Are you aware that she's _____ _____ _____ _____ (dedicated herself to the support of) the Gray Panthers?"

Dad: "Oh, my god. It's finally happened. So that's what was behind her laying claim to the old Dodge I _____ _____ _____ _____ (bought extremely cheaply) a few weeks ago. She'd been after me to get a second car for months and I'd been arguing that we were having enough difficulty _____ _____ _____ (meeting expenses), but at that price even I couldn't resist. I was hoping that having the car would _____ _____ _____ _____ _____ _____ (serve in more ways than one). Now that she's got a chance to pursue her interests, maybe she won't mind if I go ahead with my own project and panel the den. I guess the moment is opportune, and I'd better _____ _____ _____ _____ _____ _____ (make quick use of the opportunity). But since Mom's been so opposed to making changes on the house, I'll still need your help to convince her that re-doing the den is a good idea. I would really appreciate it if you'd _____ _____ _____ _____ _____ _____ _____ (apply maximum pressure to) her so I can finally get that project off the ground. Will you do that?"

Son: "Dad, I always thought you _____ _____ _____ _____ _____ (were in control of) all the big decisions around here. And now you need my help? You wouldn't have been bluffing half the time, would you?"

Dad: "No, no, you know that whenever there is something really important, I insist on my way and _____ _____ _____ _____ (do my utmost) to do it the way I think it ought to be done. But this isn't important enough to discomfort Mom. On the other hand, if she's set on joining that group and going to meetings and all, maybe I can _____ _____ _____ (insist on my course of action) when it comes to my special hobby of doing an occasional bit of carpentry. What do you think?"

Son: "Well, she can't object to the costs involved. You won't need to touch what you've _____ _____ _____ _____ _____ (set aside financially) since you've got a garage full of power tools and might as well _____ _____ _____ _____ (get the most out of them) by putting them to some good use once again. I think she's only concerned about the mess the basement will be in for months to come. But don't worry, Dad, I think you deserve a bit of fun, too, so when the time comes, I'll help _____ _____ _____ _____ _____ _____ _____ for you (extricate you from difficulties)."

Dad: "Gee, I appreciate that. After all, I'm not one to spend money foolishly, or to _____ _____ _____ _____ (go on a wild spree) or anything like that. And if I promise to keep the sawdust out of the upstairs, I'm sure Mom will come around, too, with a little support from you. And besides, I don't go around joining some darned fool enterprise like the Gray Panthers, do I?"

Son: "Oh, oh, Dad, you'd better not use that argument with Mom if you're planning to _____ _____ _____ _____ (be victorious) as far as your pet project is concerned. I'm sure she takes that as seriously as you do improving the house."

Dad: "Yes, of course you're right. That wouldn't be smart at all. I do want you to be there when I broach the subject, though, so you can keep me out of trouble. Well, I guess I'll run down to the lumberyard and start pricing the supplies I'll need. That ought to _____ _____ _____ _____ (initiate action)."

Son: "O.K., Dad. Say hello to old George down there if you see him. Is he still helping out with the business?"

Dad: "Helping out? Are you kidding? That old man _____ as _____ _____ _____ _____ _____ (entrenched) as he ever was and still makes most of the decisions. It's hard on his children because he just refuses to modernize. I can tell you, the way it's going, they won't _____ the business _____ _____ _____ _____ _____ _____ _____ (presented to them effortlessly)."

Son: "You certainly _____ _____ _____ - _____ (made an appropriate point) there, Dad. But I've heard that as soon as their father turns 75, they're going to _____ _____ _____ _____ _____ _____ (face the issue squarely) and try to talk him into retiring. He won't have to worry about the business. They are all hard workers and really _____ _____ _____ _____ _____ _____ (apply themselves assiduously), and they have made the business prosper over the years. In the end I think he'll agree that they deserve to _____ _____ _____ (assume control) and he'll learn to enjoy retirement, just as you do, Dad."

Dad: "Well, I'll enjoy it much more once we've talked Mom into my re-doing the den. And we'd better do it fast before those Gray Panthers turn her into a tiger!

* * * * *

UNIT 6 SITUATION FIT

1. There goes your sweetheart. See, right over there. If you're quick, you can still catch up with her.

    Right. Might as well _____ now and apologize to her before I lose my courage again.

2. Looks like another beautiful weekend. How about taking advantage of the weather for a trip to the canyons?

    Oh, I'd love to, but we just can't afford the added expense this month, you know. I'm having a hard enough time already_____.

3. I think your folks are finally beginning to accept me. Our relationship has never been better.

   If you feel that way, how about _____ all that good will? I'll ask them if they'll let us use their cabin in the mountains.

4. Do you think you've gotten acquainted with our procedures sufficiently to take over the office for a few days?

   You go on ahead. I feel I _____ all matters that count by now, so there shouldn't be any problem.

5. The party is in disarray. We need a strong man to take over. Why not offer the leadership to the junior representative? He's energetic and totally committed.

   Yes, but he's got a mind of his own. As soon as he has _____ _____, he'll make all sorts of changes, and then he'll have the power to see them through.

6. You really feel strongly about a downtown free of parking meters, don't you? At least I've never seen you so wrought up about anything.

   You bet I'm wrought up. In fact, I'm ready to _____ that issue, I feel so strongly about it, and I tell you why: we merchants should be making money downtown, not the city.

7. I can't believe it - I paid all the bills and there's money left over. Now we can get that new couch.

   The old one will do for a while longer. How about taking that money and _____? We've got to think of the future.

8. Any chance of replacing the chairman of the board? He's getting on toward retirement age, isn't he?

   That may be so, but I'm afraid he's _____ and wouldn't think of budging voluntarily.

9. Whatever happened to that petition your class presented you with? Did you give in to them?

    Not in the least. They could have _____ and I wouldn't have budged, and besides, I had the regulations on my side.

10. Those rosebushes out front are terrific. I bet they set you back a small fortune.

    Not at all. I _____ down at Flower City. They're on special all week, in case you want to take advantage of the opportunity yourself.

11. I don't see how you're going to get all those things done. It'll take you three weekends to get through all of that.

    Not if I really _____ for once and get those chores behind me.

12. Boy, Dad's sure in a good mood right now. When I asked him if I could have my own party in the basement this Friday, he said yes just like that.

    Really? In that case I'm going to ask about that slumber party. You've got to _____, and this seems to be the right time.

13. Can you give me a hand for a couple of weeks, Henry? I'm so far behind in my work, I don't know which way to turn first.

    That's just like you. You let it get that bad and then you expect someone else to _____ for you and straighten out your problems.

14. You're right that there is nothing the matter with this hamburger. It's so bad it can't even be considered a hamburger.

    Well, you _____ with your remark that it isn't a hamburger. And what's more, it's sloppy.

15. Look, if we're having people over, why not invite our neighbors? They're a fun couple, and I think we could be friends with them.

Great idea. We would get to know them better, and we could try to interest them in joining our baby-sitting pool. That would be a nice way to _____ _____.

16. We'll have to come up with some advance strategy for the meeting with the 'Concerned Citizens Action Group'. Any ideas what their demands are this time?

    They want to get the new tax levy rescinded, and the way they operate, they'll _____ the issue, so we'd better brace ourselves.

17. I'll take the collection box if nobody else wants to make the first move. That'll _____, anyway.

    That's great of you, really. All it usually takes is for one person to take the initiative.

18. Look at your son. It's almost noon and he's still snoozing, with clothes strewn all over the room.

    After the way he and his buddies_____ last night, it wouldn't surprise me if he didn't get up at all today. They sure did a lot of celebrating.

19. Well, are you moving to Seattle or did Gloria talk you out of it after all?

    She used every argument she could think of, but I was able to _____ _____. The job comes first, after all.

20. I don't see how Betty can miss being elected beauty queen. She's so pretty and cute.

    She was a finalist last year and it would surprise me too if she didn't _____ _____ this year.

21. I aced every one of my qualifying exams, so I don't see how I can miss out on that scholarship now, unless I do something really stupid.

    Don't worry, with your usual good luck you'll have it _____ _____. Of course it helps to be smart, too.

Idioms to choose from:

take up arms for s.t.
get s.t. for a song
make both ends meet
kill two birds with one stone
strike while the iron is hot
bring all one's guns to bear on s.t.
have a firm grip on s.t.
move heaven and earth
stand one's ground
save s.t. for a rainy day
cash in on s.t.
pull the chestnuts out of the fire
paint the town red
carry off the palm
start the ball rolling
be in the driver's seat
have s.t. handed to one on a silver platter
hit the bull's-eye
take the bull by the horns
put one's shoulder to the wheel
take the reins

UNIT 7 TEST YOURSELF

1. So what if the neighbors forgot to forward our mail. Let's
    a) not make a big issue of it
    b) not put it in cold storage
    c) not shout it from the rooftops
    d) make no bones about it

2. Tax returns are due next week. Wouldn't it be better if you did yours now rather than
    a) put it on the shelf?
    b) drop out of sight?
    c) put up a fierce resistance?
    d) put it in cold storage?

3. After the big row he had with his family last week, George decided to ... for a while until things cooled down.
    a) put up a fierce resistance
    b) wash his hands of the matter
    c) bring things under one roof
    d) drop out of sight

4. The Noltons want to emigrate to Australia. They're selling their farm and
    a) treading on delicate ground
    b) burning their bridges behind them
    c) seeing how the land lies
    d) venturing into the lion's den

5. I'd like to visit Jan this weekend, but I don't know if she's still mad at me. Maybe I'd better call her and
    a) be on my guard
    b) put all my eggs in one basket
    c) see how the land lies
    d) drop out of sight

6. That's a wonderful design, but I think you should ... until its time is ripe.
    a) put it on the shelf
    b) put it in cold storage
    c) drop out of sight
    d) be on your guard against it

7. I wouldn't volunteer to organize this year's office party if I were you. After last year's scandal, you'd be
    a) treading on delicate ground
    b) putting all your eggs in one basket
    c) making a big issue of it
    d) burning your bridges behind you

8. The landlord's been on my back ever since I moved in, and suddenly he's all smiles. Can you blame me if I
   a) make a big issue of it?
   b) make no bones about it?
   c) smell a rat?
   d) measure everything with the same yardstick?

9. I know Will failed his exams. But you needn't
   a) smell a rat
   b) try to bring everything under one roof
   c) shout it from the rooftops
   d) burn your bridges behind you

10. I refuse to be a party to such underhanded dealings. If you insist on proceeding with these negotiations in that manner, I'll
    a) measure everything with the same yardstick
    b) wash my hands of the matter
    c) venture into the lion's den
    d) tread on delicate ground

11. The rental agency is trying to evict Mrs. Fogarty for no reason at all. I hope she
    a) sees how the land lies
    b) ventures into the lion's den
    c) puts up a fierce resistance
    d) shouts it from the rooftops

12. Everybody knows how Mr. Boyd feels about Susan because he ... his admiration for her.
    a) doesn't make a big issue of
    b) makes no bones about
    c) is on his guard against
    d) puts up a fierce resistance against

13. The boss is in a bad temper. If you go and ask him for a raise now, you'll be
    a) venturing into the lion's den
    b) putting it on the shelf
    c) washing your hands of the matter
    d) smelling a rat

14. Traveling with a group of 15-year-olds is no easy task. It's difficult to
    a) wash one's hands of their plans
    b) put their plans on the shelf
    c) bring their plans under one roof
    d) put all their eggs in one basket

15. Wild rabbits are ruining gardens all over the area. The village farmers will have to
    a) be on their guard against them
    b) make no bones about them
    c) see how the land lies
    d) put them in cold storage

16. It's not fair to say that today's young people are lazy just because many of them are unemployed. You simply can't
    a) smell a rat in everybody
    b) tread on delicate ground
    c) measure everybody with the same yardstick
    d) burn your bridges behind you

17. Bobby took a big risk. He thought he could win a single-issue campaign and so he
    a) measured everything with the same yardstick
    b) put all his eggs in one basket
    c) tried to bring everything under one roof
    d) shouted it from the rooftops

* * * * *

UNIT 7 IDIOM ENTRIES AND USAGE
Individual and World (neutral)

7.1 *nicht viel Aufheben(s) von etwas machen*

   ** **not make a big issue of s.t.** **

   ** **not make a big fuss about s.t.** **

   OP: give s.o. a song and dance about s.t.
   make a big issue of s.t.
   make a big fuss about s.t.

7.2 *etwas auf die lange Bank schieben*

   ** **put s.t. on the shelf** ** /short term; procrastinate/

   But note: put s.t. in cold storage (7.6)

7.3 *von der Bildfläche verschwinden*

   ** **drop out of sight** **

   OP: appear on the scene
   But note: vanish into thin air /sudden, unexpected disappearance/

7.4 *alle Brücken hinter sich abbrechen*

   ** **burn (all) one's bridges (behind one)** **
                           boats

7.5 *(bei jdm) auf den Busch klopfen*

   ** **see how the land lies** **

   usu. NON-PAST
   * Also: find out the lay of the land
   sound s.o. out /persons/
   But note: beat around the bush /not get to the point/
                           about
   See also: jdm auf den Zahn fühlen (4.19)

7.6 *etwas auf(s) Eis legen*

put s.t. into cold storage /long term; save/

* Also: put s.t. on ice
But note: put s.t. on the shelf (7.2)

7.7 *ein heißes Eisen anfassen*

tread on delicate ground

But note: Don't wait until it's too late. Strike while the iron is hot. (6.5)

7.8 *dem Frieden nicht trauen*

smell a rat

no IMP
But note: You *can't* trust the look of things.

7.9 *etwas an die große Glocke hängen*

shout s.t. from the roof-tops

* Also: tell everybody and his brother /neutral/
Note also: He's so happy he could shout it from the roof-tops.

7.10 *seine Hände in Unschuld waschen*

wash one's hands of s.t.

Note NEG use: He's not washing his hands of the matter. /not shirking responsibility/

7.11 *sich mit Händen und Füßen gegen etwas wehren/sträuben*

put up (a) fierce resistance (against s.t.)

* Also: fight tooth and nail against s.t.

7.12 *kein Hehl aus etwas machen*

make no bones about s.t. /attitude, opinion/

IMP: Make no bones about it!
See also: kein Blatt vor den Mund nehmen (1.1)

7.13 *sich in die Höhle des Löwen begeben/wagen*

venture into the lion's den
dare (to) enter

FUT QUES: Will he dare enter the lion's den?

7.14 *etwas unter einen Hut bringen*

bring things under one roof

Example: It's difficult to bring all these factions under one roof.

7.15 *(vor etwas) auf der Hut sein*

be on one's guard (against s.t.)

7.16   *etwas über einen Kamm scheren*
   ** measure everything with the same yardstick **
   * Also: measure everything by the same standards

7.17   *alles auf eine Karte setzen*
   ** put all one's eggs in one basket **

* * * * * * *

7.18   *mit dem Feuer spielen*
   ** play with fire **

7.19   *den letzten Trumpf ausspielen*
   ** play one's last trump **

7.20   *von etwas Wind bekommen*
   ** get wind of s.t. **

* * * * *

UNIT 7   RECOGNITION

1. not make a big issue of s.t.
   a) not pay undue attention to
   b) consider not very important
   c) keep a secret
   d) inform only a select group of people

2. put s.t. on the shelf
   a) set s.t. in full view
   b) save s.t. for the future
   c) postpone s.t.
   d) consider a matter taken care of

3. drop out of sight
   a) fall off s.t.
   b) go into hiding
   c) not show up
   d) disappear

4. put s.t. into cold storage
   a) keep for some future date
   b) procrastinate about s.t.
   c) ignore s.t.
   d) pay no attention to s.t.

5. shout s.t. from the roof-tops
   a) make an announcement
   b) tell everyone about s.t.
   c) brag about s.t.
   d) be extremely happy

6. wash one's hand of s.t.
   a) pass s.t. on to s.o. else
   b) clean up after an unpleasant job
   c) ignore a pressing problem
   d) disclaim responsibility

7. put up a fierce resistance
   a) show disrespect for s.t.
   b) join an underground organization
   c) fight strongly against s.t.
   d) insulate s.t. well

8. make no bones about s.t.
   a) clearly show one's attitude
   b) refrain from telling s.t.
   c) exhibit a dislike for s.t.
   d) consider unimportant

9. venture into the lion's den
   a) try to get the biggest share
   b) become a member of a strong team
   c) go and face the enemy
   d) approach s.o. who is feared

10. bring under one roof
    a) reduce to a common formula
    b) get everyone to agree
    c) see all points of view
    d) share an apartment

11. be on one's guard against s.t.
    a) be on the alert
    b) stand watch
    c) fight against s.t.
    d) investigate s.t.

12. measure everything with the same yardstick
    a) treat as equals
    b) be fair
    c) judge by identical standards
    d) be discriminating

13. put all one's eggs in one basket
    a) pay allegiance to a single person
    b) unite several interests
    c) risk everything on one venture
    d) decide to stick with s.t.

14. burn one's bridges (behind one) _____

15. see how the land lies _____

16. tread on delicate ground _____

17. smell a rat _____

   a) distrust appearances
   b) ask s.o.'s opinion
   c) break with the past
   d) make secret arrangements
   e) do s.t. that calls for tact
   f) foil the enemy's retreat
   g) explore a situation

UNIT 7 STORY COMPLETION

Before I explain how our computer search works, Mr. Lacreebe -- oh, pardon, Mr. Lakreppe, of course -- there is this little matter of our semi-annual membership dues to settle. Ah, thank you, and here's your receipt. We do not _____ _____ _____ _____ _____ (emphasize unduly) the financial aspect here at Dear Hearts Galore, but then we do have a computer to feed, ha ha, don't we, Mr. Lakreppe. Now then, we thank you for your confidence in choosing us, and we're sure you've made a wise decision to enlist our services now. It never pays to _____ an important matter _____ _____ _____ (postpone), Mr. Lakreppe, and this is especially true when it comes to the choice of a proper mate. Just in order to avoid any of our client's _____ _____ _____ _____ (disappearing) if the first search doesn't come up with the dear heart they've been looking for, we now have weekly computer-watch evenings, and we expect all our members to sign in on a regular basis. We're not asking you to _____ _____ _____ _____ _____ (break all ties), Mr. Lakreppe, but we do think you should give your full attention to "the matter of the heart", as we like to call it.

Well, that brings me to the next point. We find that our computer watchers appreciate lots of information about a prospective date. Helps them to _____ _____ _____ _____ _____ (judge the situation), so to speak. Gives them confidence to actually meet that first computer date instead of _____ the whole matter _____ _____ _____ (postponing it indefinitely). We don't want anyone to divulge private information and we certainly don't want to _____ _____ _____ _____ (raise a sensitive issue), but we like to provide our clients with lots of data. Past experience with other agencies has made some clients a bit suspicious, and they often _____ _____ _____ (are suspicious) even where there isn't one. You can see that the questions on this little questionnaire we'd like you to fill out are straightforward and we don't go _____ your answers _____ _____ _____ (broadcasting them publicly). But we do take our responsibility seriously, and if our clients don't find a suitable match right away, we don't _____ _____ _____ _____ _____ (disclaim all responsibility); we look for the reasons. It's only very rarely that a client will _____ _____ _____ _____ _____ (object violently) about revealing details of his or her personal history, and once we assure them that all information is entirely confidential, Mr. Lakreppe, they usually _____ _____ _____ _____ _____ (reveal candidly)

the reasons for their past disappointments. Only Dear Hearts Galore will be privy
to such background information, so why don't we ___ ___ ___ ___
___ (face the difficulties squarely) right now, Mr. Lakreepe, and fill out the
questionnaire together. That way we can try to ___ your interests ___
___ ___ (combine successfully) with those of a lady candidate in our program. Of course, I understand your possible suspicions about some of these
fly-by-night computer dating outfits, Mr. Lakreppe, but you may rest at ease
with Dear Hearts Galore. We are ever ___ ___ ___ ___ (fully alert
to the danger of) the wrongful use of our data, you know. When it comes to
matters of the heart, Mr. Lakreppe, in our business you simply can't ___
___ ___ ___ ___ ___ (apply identical standards). You needn't
feel that you're ___ ___ ___ ___ ___ ___ ___ (risking
everything in a single attempt) by letting us represent you exclusively. As I said,
we are the largest agency in the field and will continue to serve you until you meet
your very own dear heart. Here on this line, please list your present net salary,
and down below there is ample space for you to provide details about all aspects
of the current value of your estate. You just give me the figures and I'll take care
of everything else for you, Mr. Lakreppe. Nothing to it at all.

* * * * *

UNIT 7 SITUATION FIT

1. Are you sure you want to change professions? I mean, it's a serious step. You could just take a vacation and think about it so that you would be free to come back if you wanted to.

    No, I don't believe in half measures. I want to get out of it altogether and
    _____. A clean break is always best.

2. That is a splendid market analysis, Will. I wonder if this could be combined
    with some of the facts and figures I've jotted down in preparation for the
    stockholders' meeting. Could you take a look at all of it and tell me if there
    is a way to _____ things _____ in my report?

    Sure can try. I see a number of connections already, so it shouldn't be too hard to find a common denominator for all the indices. Let me take this with me and I'll be back to you about it.

3. What's the last word on the new pool? Are they going to raise a new bond issue and finally get around to building it?

   The last I heard they _____. They figure the old pool could be fixed up for a lot less money and will be as good as new again.

4. It's those communists who cause all the trouble. And the Sierra Club. If they get their way, we'll be out of electricity before the end of the century.

   You must think it's all a plot, but to connect the Sierra Club, a perfectly legal organization protecting our environment, with the communists is to _____. You couldn't oversimplify the problem more.

5. I haven't seen your roommate in ages. He's never here when I drop by.

   He said something about being sick of it all one day and just got into his car and left. Since then he's _____ completely. I wonder if he'll ever be back.

6. O.k., your job is to stand here at this gate and to tear the ticket stubs. But _____ gate crashers. None of the matinee tickets are good today.

   Don't worry, I'll handle it. I've done this sort of thing before, don't you remember?

7. Well, fellow, how's the world been treating you lately? Looks like you gained about a ton, to be honest.

   Watch it, just watch it, Steve. You're _____ there. I tell you what: you don't mention this guy's weight, and I won't say anything about your bald pate, o.k.?

8. Well, Mom, you're looking at one of next year's new cheerleaders. I made it! How about that?

   I'm glad for you, of course, but as you know I _____ my concern for your school work, which is sure to suffer.

9. I was afraid my teacher would give me hell for not having turned in my report on time, but I guess she's forgotten about it.

   No, I don't think so. She's just pretty easy-going and _____ _____ assignments and stuff. That's what I like about her.

10. Let's sneak down to the bowling alley and play a couple of games, what do you say?

    If the girls find out, they'll be mad. But I bet they're ready to come along. Let me just ask them in an indirect way and _____.

11. What do you have all these savings accounts for, considering the little we've got saved? You must have an account with every bank in town.

    Just let me handle it, will you? It's just not a good idea to _____ _____. What if one of those banks goes broke?

12. Well, shall we go down to the business school and enroll you for the fall? Are you ready to sign up there?

    Yes and no. Would it be all right to _____ for another week while I think about it some more? I may decide to go to college after all.

13. I'm just going over to Ed's for a minute. I want to know how he intends to settle with me concerning the little accident in the driveway.

    Don't. There's no sense talking to him. He's turned an accident report in to his insurance company, and so he's _____. Better get in touch with that company instead.

14. I had the feeling that sales representative was pushing his own company's investment fund a bit too hard. He kept coming back to it. I wonder whether I should invest in it after all.

    Come on, don't be so suspicious. It would be natural for him to push his own company's issues. You're too ready to _____, and you forget he's never steered us wrong in the past.

15. What are you doing here? Do you want to see the Dean too?

   Yes, I finally got up my courage and followed his summons. I wonder what it's all about - surely nothing pleasant. Well, I'm next. Time for me to _____ _____. See you later.

16. Ginny's pregnant again. Have you heard?

   You're only the fifth one to tell me today. She must be _____ _____, the way that bit of news is travelling.

17. Well, how did my little fellow do, doctor? Was he brave when you pulled that old tooth?

   Well, it's out, anyway, although it took quite some persuasion to give him a shot first. He said that no cowboy ever had to have a shot first. I was surprised that he _____ to the idea of a shot rather than to the actual pulling.

Idioms to choose from:

not make a big issue of s.t.
put s.t. on the shelf
drop out of sight
burn one's bridges behind one
see how the land lies
put s.t. into cold storage
tread on delicate ground
smell a rat
shout s.t. from the roof-tops
wash one's hands of s.t.
put up a fierce resistance
make no bones about s.t.
venture into the lion's den
bring s.t. under one roof
be on one's guard against s.t.
measure everything with the same yardstick
put all one's eggs in one basket

UNIT 8 TEST YOURSELF

1. Unless you want to be charged with hit-and-run driving, you'd better ... and turn yourself in to the police.

   a) swallow the bitter pill
   b) bury your head in the sand
   c) feather your nest
   d) add fuel to the fire

2. By lending your neighbor your car without making sure when he will return it, you've really

   a) added fuel to the flames
   b) let yourself in for something
   c) thrown a monkey wrench into the works
   d) conjured up the devil

3. I finally talked my boss into giving me a raise, but for a long time I felt as though I was

   a) tilting at windmills
   b) letting myself in for it
   c) running into a brick wall
   d) putting the cart before the horse

4. If Karen thinks I'll lend her money for tap-dancing lessons, she's

   a) beating her head against a wall
   b) making a mess of things
   c) got something up her sleeve
   d) on the wrong track

5. There was no way Lucy could change her husband's mind. Trying to convince him was just like

   a) burying her head in the sand
   b) beating her head against a wall
   c) running into a brick wall
   d) creeping away with her tail between her legs

6. Bruce's chances for re-election are nil, but he thinks if he ... the problems will go away.

   a) feathers his nest
   b) rams his head against a wall
   c) buries his head in the sand
   d) swallows the bitter pill

7. When Ralph tried to fix his car himself, he

   a) was on the wrong track
   b) hoisted the white flag
   c) threw a monkey wrench into the works
   d) made a mess of things

8. With Nancy mad at you already, I wouldn't ask her sister for a date. You would just be

    a) adding fuel to the fire
    b) throwing a monkey wrench into the works
    c) conjuring up the devil
    d) on the wrong track

9. First let me get the promotion and then we'll look for a house, o.k.? Let's not

    a) let ourselves in for anything
    b) make a mess of things
    c) put the cart before the horse
    d) hoist the white flag

10. "We'll win hands down," the boys had bragged. When their team lost the game, they

    a) swallowed the bitter pill
    b) crept away with their tails between their legs
    c) buried their heads in the sand
    d) tilted at windmills

11. The delegation simply walked out of the negotiation session. And that one day before the deadline! If they didn't

    a) throw a monkey wrench into the works!
    b) put the cart before the horse!
    c) run into a brick wall!
    d) tilt at windmills!

12. If we accepted a reward in this case, they would just accuse us of

    a) running into a brick wall
    b) adding fuel to the flames
    c) having something up our sleeves
    d) feathering our own nest

13. I don't like the way these guys behind us keep following us. I'm afraid they

    a) will conjure up the devil
    b) have something up their sleeve
    c) are on the wrong track
    d) will creep away with their tail between their legs

14. No matter how that shady character tried to fight the Internal Revenue Service, it kept closing in on him and he finally had to ... in resignation.

    a) swallow the bitter pill
    b) beat his head against a brick wall
    c) creep away with his tail between his legs
    d) hoist the white flag

15. Stop talking about having a flat tire in this rain! Don't

    a) feather your nest
    b) hoist the white flag
    c) conjure up the devil
    d) put the cart before the horse

16. You may as well stop fighting the bureaucracy. It's futile and you would only be

    a) tilting at windmills
    b) making a mess of things
    c) creeping away with your tail between your legs
    d) having something up your sleeve

* * * * *

UNIT 8 IDIOM ENTRIES AND USAGE
Individual and World (negative)

8.1 *in den sauren Apfel beißen*

** swallow the bitter pill **

FUT usu. with *have to* : You'll have to swallow the bitter pill.
IMP usu. one of the following: Go and face the music!
                               Make the best of a bad bargain!
                               Grin and bear it!
* Also: face the music /*i.e., a negative reaction from s.o.*/
         make the best of a bad bargain
         grin and bear it /*chiefly exclamatory use: We'll just have to grin and bear it!*/

8.2 *sich etwas einbrocken*

** let oneself in for s.t. **

8.3 *auf Granit beißen*

** run into a brick wall **

8.4 *auf dem Holzweg sein*

** be on the wrong track **

* Also: bark up the wrong tree
But note: be off the beaten track /*at an unfrequented location*/

8.5 *mit dem Kopf durch die Wand wollen*

** ram one's head against a wall **
** beat

But note: Don't beat your head against *the* wall!
          He beat his brains out trying to remember. (cf. 1.10)

8.6 *den Kopf in den Sand stecken*

** bury one's head in the sand **
** hide

8.7 *Mist bauen*

** make a mess of things **

8.8   *Öl ins Feuer giessen*

   ** add fuel to the flames **
                        fire **

   * Also: fan the flames /intentional/
   OP: pour oil on (the) troubled waters

8.9   *das Pferd beim Schwanz aufzäumen*

   ** put the cart before the horse **

8.10   *wie ein begossener Pudel (davonschleichen)*

   ** (creep away) with one's tail between one's legs

8.11   *Sand ins Getriebe streuen*

   ** throw a monkey wrench into the works **

   IMP usu. NEG

8.12   *sein Schäfchen ins Trockene bringen*

   ** feather one's nest **

   IMP: Look out for yourself!
   * Also: look out for Number One
   But note: line one's own pocket /usu. dishonestly/

8.13   *etwas im Schilde führen*

   ** have s.t. up one's sleeve **

8.14   *die Segel streichen*

   ** hoist   the white flag **
   ** run up

   IMP: Lay down your arms!
   * Also: lay down one's arms
               show the white flag

8.15   *den Teufel an die Wand malen*

   ** conjure up the devil **

   But note: {Speak of the devil (and he appears)!
                Talk
               /exclamation when someone being talked about appears unexpectedly/

8.16   *gegen Windmühlen kämpfen*

   ** tilt at windmills **

* * * * * * *

8.17   *den Ast absägen, auf dem man sitzt*

   ** saw off the branch one is sitting on **

8.18 *Haare spalten*
       ** split hairs (over s.t.) **

8.19 *die bittere Pille schlucken*
       ** swallow the bitter pill (cf.8.1) **

* * * * *

UNIT 8 RECOGNITION

1. swallow the bitter pill   _____
2. let oneself in for s.t.   _____
3. run into a brick wall   _____
4. creep away with one's tail
   between one's legs   _____

   a) get into difficulties
   b) be insulted
   c) accept unpleasant consequences
   d) be dejected
   e) surmount all obstacles
   f) meet strong resistance

5. be on the wrong track   _____
6. ram one's head against a wall   _____
7. bury one's head in the sand   _____
8. make a mess of things   _____

   a) do s.t. all wrong
   b) try hard to remember
   c) be mistaken
   d) face opposition courageously
   e) ignore difficulties
   f) try in vain to force an issue

9. add fuel to the flames
   a) make a situation worse
   b) try to get people interested
   c) make a big commotion about s.t.
   d) enliven the festivities

10. put the cart before the horse
    a) make life easier for s.o.
    b) misunderstand the true nature of s.t.
    c) do things in the wrong sequence
    d) mix up cause and effect

11. throw a monkey wrench into
    the works
    a) cause people to take notice
    b) use one's influence
    c) give up on a project
    d) interfere with s.t.

12. feather one's nest
   a) aggrandize oneself
   b) build a home
   c) make life easier for oneself
   d) get an easy job

13. have s.t. up one's sleeve
   a) cheat in a card game
   b) be untrustworthy
   c) have something saved for the future
   d) plan some secret action

14. hoist the white flag
   a) celebrate
   b) give up
   c) claim victory
   d) give the start signal

15. conjure up the devil
   a) take part in secret rites
   b) wish someone evil
   c) portray s.t. unpleasant
   d) mention s.o. and he appears

16. tilt at windmills
   a) engage in sporting events
   b) give in to opposition
   c) fight against insurmountable odds
   d) look foolish

* * * * *

UNIT 8 STORY COMPLETION

A: Look, if you really can't get both term papers finished, it's probably best to _____ _____ _____ _____ (accept the situation) and take an incomplete for the course.

B: Yeah, but that means I would have to finish the other one next term, and I'll be snowed under with practice teaching then, so I would really _____ _____ _____ _____ _____ it (get myself in difficulty). I just don't think I could handle it all. Do you think I could get a two-week extension and hand in Professor Brian's paper after finals?

A: Trying to get anything out of that prof is like _____ _____ _____ _____ _____ (facing an impenetrable barrier), believe me. Don't even ask. He wouldn't give you the time of day, as tough as he is.

B: I don't think he's all that bad. No, I think you _____ _____ _____ _____ _____ (are decidedly mistaken) there; actually, he can be quite nice. Maybe I will try it and ask him nicely. Perhaps if I explain ...

A: Well, if you insist on _____ _____ _____ _____ _____ _____ (going up against impossible odds), go right ahead. Don't say I didn't warn you, though. If you ignore this man's fierce reputation, you're just _____ _____ _____ _____

_____ _____ *(refusing to face facts)*. Just think what a _____ _____ _____
_____ _____ *(difficulties you'll create)!* You know the stories of how he picks
on people in class once he gets to know their names. Besides, you'll be _____
_____ _____ _____ _____ *(worsening the situation gravely)* for the next
semester, when you have to take his other course. He's the only one who teaches
the survey courses, don't forget.

B: Oh, I forgot about that second course. You may be right after all. I'd better
not draw his attention or he'll murder me next year, especially since he's got this
hang-up about how his assignments take priority over everyone else's. I see that
I would be _____ _____ _____ _____ _____ _____ *(doing things backwards)*
if I entered his line of vision during the first term already. And he's supposed to
be even tougher in the follow-up course. What am I going to do?

A: Well, there's no need to _____ _____ _____ _____ _____ _____ _____
_____ *(feel totally dejected)*, either. What if you take an incomplete in Physical
Education? Would that _____ _____ _____ _____ _____ _____ _____
(block things terribly) as far as scheduling goes?

B: No, that wouldn't be the problem, but the coach would be mad. I'm supposed
to be playing on the team next fall, but the P.E. prerequisite has to be completed
for me to be eligible. However, that's the lesser evil at the moment. Might as well
_____ _____ _____ *(look to my own advantage)* in this instance and not worry
about the team.

A: Atta boy! But you better think up some darn good excuse for the coach. He
knows you're hooked on football and wouldn't give it up unless you _____ _____
_____ _____ _____ *(are planning some scheme)*. I mean you're not known to
_____ _____ _____ _____ _____ *(give up)* down on the field, no matter how
tough the opponent. What if he starts grilling you about your reasons for dropping
out, or gets hold of your midterm grades or something? Did you think of that? If
he finds out what's behind all this, he'll lower the boom on you. You know the
coach, ha ha.

B: Oh, wow, don't even mention it, you shouldn't _____ _____ _____ _____
(bring up possible disasters) that way! Oh boy oh boy oh boy, am I in hot water.
What now?

A: Easy. Stop guzzling beer every night, cut down on your dating, and get to
work for once. If you really hustle, you can still get both term papers in before
the deadline. When it comes right down to it, there is no way to fight the system,
you're bound to lose. We're wise to you guys, we've heard it all. If you try out
your windy excuses, you'll just be _____ _____ _____ *(fighting impossible*

battles), believe you me.

B: Gee, Mr. Brown, you know, you're a regular guy. You keep me to the straight and narrow. Best advisor I ever did have!

* * * * *

UNIT 8   *SITUATION FIT*

1. I'm going to do everything I can to delay the road construction until we have assurances that the housing development will be built.

    Listen, Crabtree, if you are going to _____ at this point and run the risk of having the housing company back out, we'll hold you personally responsible. Everything is set, and we need no interference from you.

2. Is Sylvia mad about something? She walked by me without even saying hello.

    She let her driver's license expire, and now she has to _____
    _____ and go through all of that examination process again. And she hates memorizing traffic rules!

3. We've got to reason with our youngest. He's dead set to build that house even though he's got no financing for it.

    Let him _____ if he wants to. As soon as he talks to the loan officer at the bank, he'll find out he won't be able to get his way this time.

4. I almost feel sorry for Dick. That girl was really hard on him.

    Yes, I felt sorry for him too, the way he _____. I wish he would assert himself more. After all, he meant well.

5. Now that they squelched public debate and even took the whole issue off the ballot, they think they have the problem solved.

    They should have known that such retrenching would have the opposite effect and would only _____. Now the situation is worse than ever.

6. I'll make the city council come around to my way of thinking yet. Did you see the latest petition I put in?

   Forget it. You're _____. Your proposals are much too far out to ever get any support.

7. That country is in trouble and nearly broke. What happened to the former dictator there?

   Oh, he's long gone, and with him went a fair share of the national wealth. He made sure to _____ and probably has numbered bank accounts everywhere now.

8. This house-watching for my aunt and uncle while they are on vacation has turned into a lot of work. There's a dog to walk, fish to be fed, and about a thousand flowers to water.

   It's unlike you to _____ something like this, but since they are your relatives, you can hardly get around it.

9. This is what the government gets for years of neglect. Now the problem has ballooned all out of proportion.

   You're so right. Problems just don't go away when you _____. What we need is action.

10. You wouldn't have taken my overnight bag by any chance, would you? I can't find it anywhere, and you're the last one to have taken a trip.

    Sorry, bud, but if you're looking my way for that bag, you're _____. You seem to forget that you just cleaned out your closet and probably put it away somewhere.

11. Let's not go down this block. I don't like the looks of these guys at the other end. We can turn left here instead.

    Hurry up. They're looking at us. I suspect they _____ or they wouldn't give us the eye like that. I'm scared.

12. Let's just get everything off the truck and into the house first, and we'll worry about how to arrange the furniture later.

   That would be _____. We'd have a house full of stuff which has to be rearranged, and it will be too crowded to even move. Why not decide where everything goes beforehand?

13. I thought you were getting married? You've been engaged for some time now, haven't you?

   Don't even remind me. You know Jim - trying to talk that guy into anything he isn't ready for is like _____. He's got his own ideas and won't deviate from them for anything.

14. I'm worried about the kids. They said they would be here before sundown. What if they had an accident?

   Don't _____. You panic every time they're late. They're adults now, don't forget.

15. Oops, forgot about the undercoating. Can we do without it?

   You must be out of your mind. That would really _____. Latex paint without an undercoating would peel off in no time.

16. Give me a drink, quick. I've asked your sister to marry me for the last time. She's turned me down again.

   You're wise to _____ when it comes to proposing to my sister. She's just not the marrying kind.

Idioms to choose from:

swallow the bitter pill
let oneself in for s.t.
run into a brick wall
be on the wrong track
ram one's head against a wall
bury one's head in the sand
make a mess of things
add fuel to the flames

put the cart before the horse
creep away with one's tail between one's legs
throw a monkey wrench into the works
feather one's nest
have s.t. up one's sleeve
run up the white flag
conjure up the devil
tilt against windmills

UNIT 9 TEST YOURSELF

1. Talk to Milly when she stops by tonight and ask her for a date. If you don't, you'll let a fine opportunity

   a) take the cake
   b) go down the drain
   c) be a godsend
   d) be touch and go

2. It may have been true once that our team was the greatest. But now, after yet another loss, it looks like

   a) the tables are turned
   b) that is water over the dam
   c) that's not worth a tinker's damn
   d) that stinks to high heaven

3. Our son has failed organic chemistry three times now and with that his chances to become a doctor are over.

   a) That takes the cake.
   b) That's no picnic.
   c) That's the upshot of the matter.
   d) That happens only once in a blue moon.

4. I don't know why our neighbor must mow his lawn every Sunday morning. And do you see that? He's dumping his cuttings into our bushes.

   a) That takes the cake!
   b) That's the upshot of the matter!
   c) That sets a precedent!
   d) That spreads like wildfire!

5. A refund from the Internal Revenue Service!

   a) It goes without saying.
   b) It's six of one and half-a-dozen of the other.
   c) It goes down the drain.
   d) It's a godsend.

6. I know we forgot to wish your brother a happy birthday. But that was weeks ago.

   a) That is water over the dam.
   b) It won't cost an arm and a leg.
   c) It's the talk of the town.
   d) The tables are turned.

7. We're living way beyond our means, so ... that we have to start saving money.

   a) it happens only once in a blue moon
   b) it stinks to high heaven
   c) it's no bed of roses
   d) it goes without saying

8. The washer you bought at the garage sale has broken down again. I told you it would
    a) be no bed of roses
    b) go without saying
    c) not cost an arm and a leg
    d) not be worth a damn

9. Jack has worked for that company for 25 years and just before he could retire they fired him, so they won't have to pay him any retirement benefits. If that doesn't
    a) stink to high heaven!
    b) go down the drain!
    c) set a precedent!
    d) cost an arm and a leg!

10. Mabel doesn't have it easy. Not only does she hold down a full-time job, but she has that big household to take care of, too. You know yourself that that's
    a) the upshot of the matter
    b) no bed of roses
    c) touch and go
    d) the talk of the town

11. I don't care if you do your homework first and then clean your room or the other way around.
    a) It happens only once in a blue moon.
    b) That takes the cake.
    c) It's six of one and half-a-dozen of the other.
    d) That is a godsend.

12. We'd better be grateful that your sister has offered to babysit for us.
    a) That spreads like wildfire.
    b) It's the talk of the town.
    c) That is water over the damn.
    d) That happens only once in a blue moon.

13. Maybe Bill will be admitted to college, and maybe he won't.
    a) It's touch and go.
    b) The tables are turned.
    c) It's not worth a damn.
    d) It's six of one and half-a-dozen of the other.

14. I'm sure we can get unemployment benefits if Beth got them. After all, the decision in her case
    a) was a godsend
    b) set a precedent
    c) happened only once in a blue moon
    d) took the cake

15. Jack had an affair with some girl at work, and by now
    a) it has spread like wildfire
    b) it's the talk of the town
    c) the tables are turned
    d) that's the upshot of the matter

16. Come on, let's take up tennis. After all,

    a) it won't cost an arm and a leg
    b) it won't go down the drain
    c) it will be touch and go
    d) it will set a precedent

17. The news that the tractor plant will expand its facilities here has gotten out prematurely. That kind of information was bound to

    a) be water over the dam
    b) not be worth a tinker's damn
    c) spread like wildfire
    d) set a precedent

* * * * *

UNIT 9   IDIOM ENTRIES AND USAGE
Focus on the World

9.1   *in die Binsen gehen*

    ** go down the drain **

    * Also: come to nothing /expectations/
                go up in smoke /expectations/
                go to pot /e.g. business, objects/
                fall through /e.g. trips/

9.2   *das Blatt hat sich gewendet*

    ** the tables are turned **

    restr. to above form
    * Also: the tide has turned
                the shoe is on the other foot /change in roles/
    But note: turn over a new leaf /change one's conduct/
                turn the tables /reverse conditions/

9.3   *das Ende vom Lied sein*

    ** that's the upshot of the matter **

    negative (or neutral) remark
    But note: That's the end of the matter. Don't bother me with it anymore.

9.4   *das schlägt dem Faß den Boden aus!*

    ** that takes the cake! **

    restr. to PRES and NEG QUES.
    Example: Doesn't that take the cake?
    * Also: be the limit

9.5   *ein Geschenk des Himmels sein*

    ** be a godsend **

9.6 *über etwas ist längst Gras gewachsen*

    ** that is water over the dam ** /statement/
                       under the bridge ** /statement/

    * Also: s.t. is dead and buried
                  let bygones be bygones /usu. exhortation/

9.7 *etwas liegt (klar) auf der Hand*

    ** it goes without saying ** /foregone conclusion/

usu. followed by *that*
alternative pattern: *that ... without saying*
Examples: It goes without saying that rain is wet.
              That rain is wet goes without saying.
no PROG. usu. PRES
* Also: s.t. is as plain as {can be /self-evident/
                          {day
But note: have s.t. on hand /available/

9.8 *keinen roten Heller wert sein*

    ** not worth a (tinker's) damn **

9.9 *zum Himmel stinken/schreien*

    ** stink to high heaven **

no PROG

9.10 *das ist kein Honiglecken!*

    ** s.t. is no bed of roses ** /condition/

    * Also: s.t.'s no picnic! /activity/
    OP: that's easy sledding!
                that's a piece of cake!

9.11 *das ist Jacke wie Hose*

    ** it's six of one and half-a-dozen of the other **

9.12 *nur alle Jubeljahre einmal vorkommen*

    ** happen (only) once in a blue moon **

    Examples: That doesn't happen only once in a blue moon;
                   it occurs quite frequently.
                 Once in a blue moon you can find a really good buy there.

9.13 *auf der Kippe stehen*

    ** be touch and go **

But note: be on the brink /in a precarious situation/

9.14 *etwas macht Schule*

    ** s.t. sets a precedent **

9.15 *die Spatzen pfeifen es von den Dächern*

** it's the talk of the town **

But note: shout s.t. from the roof-tops (7.9)

9.16 *etwas wird die Welt nicht kosten*

** s.t. won't cost an arm and a leg **

OP: cost a pretty penny /much/
cost an arm and a leg /too much/

But note: cost next to nothing /be inexpensive/

9.17 *sich mit Windeseile verbreiten*

** spread like wildfire **

* * * * * * *

9.18 *auf fruchtbaren Boden fallen*

** fall on fertile ground **

* * * * *

UNIT 9 RECOGNITION

1. that takes the cake   _____
2. it's a godsend   _____
3. that won't cost an arm and
   a leg   _____
4. it's not worth a tinker's damn _____
5. it's six of one and half-a-dozen
   of the other   _____

        a) is not overpriced
        b) makes no difference
        c) is somewhat expensive
        d) isn't worth anything
        e) is a timely bit of good luck
        f) is easily quantified
        g) is a rude, unexpected action

6. that is water over the dam _____
7. it happens once in a blue
   moon   _____
8. s.t. goes down the drain   _____
9. it's touch and go   _____

        a) is a loss
        b) occurs rarely
        c) is past and can't be changed
        d) takes place every month
        e) has been spilled
        f) of uncertain outcome

10. the tables are turned
    a) conditions are reversed
    b) things are upside-down
    c) the restaurant is closed
    d) things have gotten worse

11. that's the upshot of the matter
    a) that's the just reward
    b) that's the final element
    c) the target has been hit
    d) that's the outcome

12. it goes without saying
    a) it isn't a secret
    b) it's obvious
    c) it can be deleted
    d) it is instrumental

13. that stinks to high heaven
    a) that's illegal
    b) it's going up in smoke
    c) it is considered an injustice
    d) it's a sin

14. s.t.'s no bed of roses
    a) an unkempt garden
    b) an uncomfortable bed
    c) not a neat arrangement
    d) not an easy life

15. sets a precedent
    a) provides a good justification
    b) comes before s.t. else
    c) can be used as a model
    d) explains the foregoing

16. it's the talk of the town
    a) everybody knows about it
    b) it is communicated rapidly
    c) it's great news
    d) it is terribly important

17. s.t. spreads like wildfire
    a) is contagious
    b) is communicated rapidly
    c) is of great magnitude
    d) is distributed everywhere

* * * * *

UNIT 9 STORY COMPLETION

O.K., Jenny, let's not let this opportunity _____ _____ _____ _____ (be lost forever). After all, now that the baby's here, _____ _____ _____ _____ (matters are reversed), and we can use the extra money. Actually, with an extra mouth to feed, we can't do without it, _____ _____ _____ _____ _____ _____ (to sum it all up). Even counting the second mortgage we've applied for, things will be tight. If the bank were to decide at the last moment to disapprove it, wouldn't that _____ _____ _____ (be the limit)? After all the years we've done business with them? Anyway, let's accept that plastic-ware distributorship you've been thinking about. If we're honest about it, _____ really _____ _____ (it's a real blessing). On the other hand, we can forget about the cosmetics contract we lost -- _____ _____ _____ _____ _____ _____ (it's behind us and finished). It _____ _____ _____ (need not be pointed out) that we'll never hear from them again. Besides, their commission schedule wasn't _____ _____ _____ (valuable in the least) in any case. Deals like that _____ _____ _____ _____ (are an outrage), if you ask me. Of course, the plastic-ware sales program will _____ _____ _____ _____ _____ (not be easy) either, but if we're going to take on extra work, it might as well be a good money-making opportunity. And as far as work expenditure is concerned, _____ _____ _____ _____ _____ - _____ - _____ _____ _____ _____ (it comes out just the same), don't you think? _____ _____ _____ _____ _____ _____ _____ _____ (It is extremely rare) that two such opportunities come up at the same time, and even though we lost one and the other was _____ _____ _____ (highly uncertain) for a while, with the contract offer we're in the clear now, the way I see it. Your father paid me a compliment, by the way. He said that the way we're striving to meet our responsibilities will _____ _____ _____ (serve as a model) for the whole family. I thought that was nice. Nevertheless, as far as the neighbors are concerned, we shouldn't let the news get out before we've actually signed the contract; soon _____ _____ _____ _____ _____ _____ _____ _____ (simply everybody will know it) anyway. Come to think of it, with all the additional driving we'll have to do, we'll also need a more reliable second car, but we should be able to find one that _____ _____ _____ _____ _____ _____ _____ (won't be excessively expensive). Naturally, that is something we can't hide from the neighbors, so that news at least will _____ _____ _____ (travel fast). You know how people gossip in this little town!

* * * * *

UNIT 9 SITUATION FIT

1. "Sis, I'm going to get a job. I just can't go on letting you pay all the bills."

    "Look, it's really quite simple. When I was laid up for a year and a half with my leg injury, you went to work and supported me. Now that I have a good job and you're finishing college, _____. I'll be glad to carry the financial responsibility for us both until you've finished."

2. "That damned air-conditioner broke down again. I'll take it into the shop on my way to work and maybe they can fix it before tonight."

   "I wouldn't even try to get it fixed. Trade it in on another one while it's still under warranty. I mean, we've discovered already that these off-brand models _____."

3. "Maybe with inflation so high it would be a good idea to renovate the house right away rather than wait as we had planned."

   "You're right. The longer we wait, the more the purchasing power of our savings will decrease. This may be our last opportunity. If we don't use our money now, it may_____."

4. "I wish you wouldn't get so worked up about the election."

   "But it was rigged! It was clearly rigged, and everybody knows it! That kind of blatant disregard of the democratic process_____!"

5. "I thought Jim wanted to take our daughter out to a movie. And now they're sitting out in the living room glued to the TV as usual. What happened?"

   "It makes me mad, too. He's always such a homebody, and now that he made definite plans to take her out, which as you know_____ _____, his car had to break down. It's a real shame."

6. "I hate to complain about the neighbors, Ted, but I think you should talk to that man, as unpleasant as it is. He acts as if our lawn is his property. Remember when he took the engine out of his junk heap and left it on our lawn for a week? He never leaves us any parking spaces out by the curb, and this afternoon I couldn't go shopping because he had parked his trailer right across our driveway. Look, it's still there!"

   "Well, I've got to admit, that _____! I'm going over there right now!"

7. "I think the block party was wonderful and made all the work that went into it worthwhile. We met so many nice people from the neighborhood. Was there ever a block party before this one?"

"No, ours was the first one ever. But since it was such a success, I'm sure it will _____. Word will get around and before long there will be block parties all over this part of town."

8. "It's now official: we'll be getting the new airport. The governor has just given his final approval."

"Well, that'll be good news to everyone, and it will bring new business to the town. Do you mind if I pass that information on to the Daily Bugle?"

"No, no, under no circumstances. News like that_____ _____ and we must leave it to the mayor to make the announcement. After all, he deserves the major credit for it all."

9. "Here you are, Mom. I've got the ladder ready. Do you want to do the front or the back windows first?"

"Well, since the sun isn't shining today, _____. We can start wherever you like, just as long as you help me."

10. "I've thought about it, and I think that Ron should be given another chance. O.K., so the accident was his fault, but he is a mature boy now, and besides, he does need a car to get to his job."

"I don't think he's mature enough at all. He already had two accidents before, and we all warned him about his driving. Now he's had another one. But we don't need to argue about it. Don't forget that his driver's license will be suspended. He'll get fined and he won't be allowed to drive at all for a while. So he'll have to take the bus to work. That, in essence, is _____ _____."

11. "Look, I know the garage doesn't really need it, but could we have it painted anyway while the men are here doing the house? It just doesn't match the color of the house at all anymore."

"I see what you mean. Let me talk to them. As they already have all their equipment here, that extra bit of work _____, so we should be able to afford it, and it will look so much better."

12. "I'm afraid I may have divulged a secret last night when I let it slip out that your boss's daughter is engaged, and now I feel really embarrassed."

    "Oh, you can rest easy on that score, Milly. The news has been around for weeks, and by now _____."

13. "I thought that Harry looked terrible when they were here last night. Is he sick or something?"

    "No, it's not that at all. The union is threatening to strike at his plant, and as chief negotiator for management he's caught between the camps. He's having a terrible time, and it's been going on for weeks now. The position he's in is certainly _____."

14. "Can you give us any assurance that the dam will hold?"

    "We can't say as of now. It all depends on how fast the snow melts upstream. We've reinforced the dam with sandbags, but the way it looks now, even without additional rainfall, it will _____."

15. "I'm really sorry I forgot to turn off the headlights last night, Dad, but it won't happen again, I promise. I suppose you'll never let me use the car again?"

    "Forget it, son. I had to let it roll down the hill a bit this morning and got it started that way, and by now the battery has recharged itself. That can happen to anyone, so don't worry about it anymore. _____ _____."

16. "Guess what came today: the new snow-blower!"

    "I was wondering how long it would take me to shovel my way out of the garage, the way it's been snowing all morning. If that didn't arrive just in time. Why, it sure _____!"

17. "Waiter, I can't eat this pizza. It's all burned on the bottom!"

    "You're absolutely right, Sir. It should never have been served that way. I'll

order another one for you right away, and we're very sorry. _____
_____ that you will not be charged for this meal. We like to keep
our customers happy!"

Idioms to choose from:

go down the drain
the tables are turned
that's the upshot of the matter
take the cake
be a godsend
that is water over the dam
it goes without saying
not worth a (tinker's) damn
s.t. stinks to high heaven
s.t.'s no bed of roses
be six of one and half-a-dozen of the other
happen (only) once in a blue moon
be touch and go
set a precedent
it's the talk of the town
won't cost an arm and a leg
s.t. spreads like wildfire

FINAL CHECK

1. I may not agree with the way Mrs. Jonas chooses to handle our applicants, but as long as she's my supervisor and I'm still on probation, she's the one who

    a) gives herself airs
    b) calls the shots
    c) grabs the bull by the horns
    d) puts in her two cents worth

2. I honestly don't know how the Clarksons do it. They're on welfare and yet they have a house, a car *and* a boat. They have so little apparent income and yet they

    a) adorn themselves with borrowed plumes
    b) are securely in the driver's seat
    c) live high off the hog
    d) bury their head in the sand

3. What annoys me about David is that he hardly ever makes a decision that might be unpopular with people who hold important positions. No matter what the issue, he checks on their opinions first to avoid

    a) putting in his two cents worth
    b) setting a precedent
    c) sticking his neck out
    d) going to bat for s.o.

4. It was apparently quite a camping trip. They lost their way in a sandstorm, had to rescue their equipment from a capsized boat, and finally were chased by a hungry grizzly bear. He had been gaining on them, but they finally reached the rangers' outpost,

    a) going on the warpath
    b) making it by the skin of their teeth
    c) making themselves scarce
    d) and drew a bead on him

5. The neighborhood boys would always play in the empty lot across the street, building bonfires and carrying on all hours of the night, no matter how much people complained. It was only when they saw the police car coming up the hill that they

    a) started the ball rolling
    b) put their shoulder to the wheel
    c) hightailed it out of there
    d) kicked the bucket

6. When we were looking for our first apartment, we inquired at an agency in a fairly fashionable area. When the agent named a rental figure that amounted to twice our monthly salaries, we ... and let her show us the apartment anyway.

    a) didn't bat an eyelash
    b) saw through her little game
    c) put all our eggs in one basket
    d) stood our ground

7. Even though Lucy couldn't stand classical music, when her new boyfriend asked her to go to a piano recital with him, she ... and accepted.

   a) beat her breast
   b) gave him moral support
   c) put a brave face on it
   d) played into his hand

8. I'm really glad you dropped by. We enjoyed seeing you and chatting about old times. I hope now that you're back in town, you won't ... anymore and come by more often.

   a) fly off the handle
   b) make yourself scarce
   c) creep away with your tail between your legs
   d) make a mess of things

9. It was clear that once Ralph took up skateboarding, all the kids on his block would too. It's obvious that in his crowd he's the one who

   a) calls the tune
   b) has s.t. up his sleeve
   c) sweeps them off their feet
   d) lets himself in for things

10. Freddy's going for a job interview tomorrow. He really wants this job and so he'll make a particular effort to ... when he's with the personnel manager.

    a) be a godsend
    b) have a firm grip on it
    c) venture into the lion's den
    d) weigh his words

11. Susan's been out playing volley-ball every afternoon and forgetting to do her homework. Apparently she doesn't know that she needs a certain average to get into her chosen college. When she finds out, she'll no doubt

    a) have things handed to her on a silver platter
    b) rack her brain
    c) change her tune
    d) put a brave face on it

12. Arthur reported that his do-it-yourself renovations were progressing well, except that every time he climbed out onto that rickety old fire escape, he felt he was

    a) taking his life in his hands
    b) on the skids
    c) not worth a tinker's damn
    d) touch and go

13. Our son was particularly friendly and helpful when new neighbors moved in down the block. As a matter of fact, I saw him doing things for them that he never does at home. This continued for a few days before ... that it must be their pretty daughter who made him so attentive.

    a) it threw a scare into me
    b) it cleared the air
    c) it was music to my ears
    d) it dawned on me

14. At first we cleaned out a closet here, painted a ceiling there, mostly evenings or weekends. But now we have two weeks' vacation and consequently our re-decorating

    a) is spreading like wildfire
    b) is on the wrong track
    c) is making us shape up
    d) is going full blast

15. If Mr. Harvey throws his garbage on our lawn one more time I'm going to go over there and tell him what I think of such behavior. And the rules of our Good Neighbors League notwithstanding, I certainly will

    a) not throw in the towel
    b) not harm a hair on his head
    c) make no bones about it
    d) not mince words

16. Now that Sheila's gotten her first book published and it met with such success, she feels that she's entitled to ... for a while.

    a) not bat an eyelash
    b) shout it from the rooftops
    c) go into a huddle
    d) rest on her oars

17. Somehow money really gets one down to the basics in life. I always thought we were such a friendly and cooperative family. But when Aunt Gerda died and left an inheritance worth fighting over, suddenly everyone

    a) showed their true colors
    b) stuck up for her
    c) tilted at windmills
    d) laughed up their sleeve

18. Life was wonderful when we were in college. We were away from home for the first time and, although we had to work hard, we were always dreaming about the future and

    a) feathering our nest
    b) building castles in the air
    c) getting s.t. for a song
    d) moving heaven and earth

19. The going will be rough for you now that you've lost your job. But I know you're a highly qualified specialist and I'm sure it won't take long before you've found another one. Just ... and cut back a little on expenditures until then.

    a) cash in on s.t.
    b) take the reins
    c) put your foot in it
    d) keep a stiff upper lip

20. That stock offer really does sound too good to be true. Thanks for bringing it to my attention. I think I'd rather ... and put my money into high-interest savings certificates, though.

    a) cash in on it
    b) play it safe
    c) pay you back in kind
    d) dance to s.o. else's tune

21. Nobody told Charlie to let the reporters in. He

   a) took them in
   b) stood his ground
   c) acted on his own authority
   d) brought them under one roof

22. Marjorie knew she'd put the book down somewhere in the house. She ... but simply couldn't remember where she'd left it.

   a) flew off the handle
   b) racked her brain
   c) went full blast
   d) tilted at windmills

23. One time he tilts this way, then again another, just as it suits him. I guess he looks toward his own advantage too much and tends to

   a) howl with the pack
   b) be six of one and half-a-dozen of the other
   c) measure everything with the same yardstick
   d) put all his eggs in one basket

24. It's a shame how Judy has given up all aspirations of getting a college degree. I think someone ought to get her out of her rut. She doesn't date, she never goes out, shows no outside interests at all, and she doesn't even bother to dress well. After all, we're her friends and later we would blame ourselves terribly if we had let her

   a) burn her bridges behind her
   b) wash her hands of it
   c) venture into the lion's den
   d) fall by the wayside

25. My conscience tells me not to take any credit for the final form of the agreement. All I did was get the parties to the bargaining table and keep them there. If I claimed anything more, I would be

   a) calling the shots
   b) resting on my oars
   c) taking my life into my hands
   d) adorning myself with borrowed plumes

26. Look, the damage is already done. There is no sense in quibbling with the past. What's done is done and can't be changed. The thing for you to do is to look toward the future and to stop

   a) breeding bad blood
   b) beating your breast
   c) putting the cart before the horse
   d) kicking the bucket

27. Well, I don't think it's as serious as all that. You're still carrying a B in your major, and you're doing o.k. in all your electives. So these five hours of D in foreign languages won't hurt your grade average that much. If you work on your grades before finals, there is absolutely no need to

   a) stick your neck out
   b) throw in the towel
   c) put a brave face on it
   d) let it pass

28. I just saw in the paper that Fred's boy has been caught stealing again. This time it was a car. At one time he was just a juvenile delinquent, but now he has a record a mile long. If he doesn't get help quick, he'll soon

    a) be on the skids
    b) show his true colors
    c) change his tune
    d) burn his bridges

29. When you talk to the school board tonight, be sure to avoid mentioning the new sex education program. It's a real thorn in the side of the principal, and all you have to do is to mention it to him and he is sure to

    a) fly off the handle
    b) call the tune
    c) swallow the bitter pill
    d) play it safe

30. It's about time we go in and rescue Mom. That insurance salesman has been in there with her for the last two hours, and you know what a pest he can be. If we don't put a stop to it, he'll just keep working on Mom to buy more insurance and will

    a) tread on delicate ground
    b) rule the roost
    c) talk her ear off
    d) see how the land lies

31. Now that Riley has finally inherited his father's fortune, he's become impossible. He has no manners and of course he doesn't have any taste, but what's worse is that, although he hasn't got half the brain his father had, he thinks that just because he has money he can look down on others and

    a) dance to someone else's tune
    b) put his shoulder to the wheel
    c) give himself airs
    d) keep a stiff upper lip

32. That loss to the Celtics last night was your last chance, coach. I'm going to have to let you go. Your psychology in getting the team "up" for the games isn't working. Even though you ..., it made no difference in the team's performance.

    a) talked yourself hoarse
    b) played right into their hands
    c) were hard on their heels
    d) put your foot in it

33. I'd forgotten that there was a can of paint on top of that sheet of plywood that I pulled down from that shelf, and although I could see the can coming and ducked, it still hit me hard enough to make

    a) it dawn on me
    b) me shape up
    c) me see stars
    d) me smell a rat

34. Let's not forget that it is only in his home district that the senator makes all these promises about increased social services to his constituents. As soon as he is back in Washington, he inevitably votes Republican. I say let's get him out of office, because he's

 a) hard on our heels
 b) weighing his words
 c) sailing under false colors
 d) not mincing words

35. They both come from broken homes, and since neither of them had finished high school, it looked like they would have a rough time of it when they got married. But now they have two lovely children and secure jobs, and they've worked miracles on their house. Just to think that we once thought their marriage would

 a) end up on the rocks!
 b) take the cake!
 c) be the talk of the town
 d) run into a brick wall

36. That McMurty was a tough old guy, and everybody thought he would live forever, but after they built the highway through his backyard and his last horse died, he got so sick that they had to put him in the hospital, and now that oldtimer has finally

 a) dropped out of sight
 b) kicked the bucket
 c) put up a fierce resistance
 d) gone down the drain

37. The body shop down on Lincoln Street got its work orders mixed up, and you should have seen Max when he went to pick up his Bug. He could hardly believe his eyes when he saw that they'd made a dune buggy out of it. Boy, did he ever

 a) hit the bull's-eye
 b) beat his head against a wall
 c) blow his stack
 d) conjure up the devil

38. Every time we think we have hammered out a contract both sides can live with, the shop stewards balk at it. This has happened so often that there must be some design behind it. We've got to stop these delaying tactics and, above all, we must tell them once and for all to stop

 a) sailing under false colors
 b) getting out of line
 c) saving for a rainy day
 d) running into a brick wall

39. These repeated budget cuts are more than upsetting the people. If there is one more sensitive issue like further cuts in the School Lunch Program, I'm afraid a lot of parents will band together and

 a) put their foot in it
 b) get in each other's hair
 c) paint the town red
 d) go on the warpath

40. It's not to your credit that you let your friend sit down in the ketchup after you had seen it drip onto the chair just so you could

    a) laugh up your sleeve
    b) carry off the palm
    c) give him a broad hint
    d) howl with the pack

41. Ever since his illness, the Dawsons are having trouble keeping up their house. He can't do the outside work anymore like he used to. And they don't have the money to hire someone to do it for them. It would be nice if you'd go and

    a) keep them up to date
    b) see how the land lies
    c) lend them a helping hand
    d) take up arms for them

42. Father always had it in for my little brother. Whenever anything went wrong in our house, he was blamed for it. The other kids would go out to get away from trouble, so I felt I at least had to stay and

    a) keep tabs on him
    b) put a brave face on it
    c) feel him out
    d) stick up for him

43. I really don't know why all the students are so afraid of their history teacher. Mr. Matthews seems so sweet and gentle. He wouldn't

    a) bat an eyelash
    b) harm a hair on anyone's head
    c) make a big issue of things
    d) throw in the towel

44. Ever since Aunt Margaret's illness, people think of her as delicate and .... They don't realize that she's the same old champion that she always was.

    a) keep her in check
    b) are on their guard against her
    c) treat her with kid gloves
    d) pull the chestnuts out of the fire for her

45. Don't worry about Philip getting his folks to lend us their new car for our trip into the back woods. He's good at ... and getting his way.

    a) ramming his head against a wall
    b) throwing dust in people's eyes
    c) making both ends meet
    d) acting on his own authority

46. John is working hard on an article and is having trouble getting his ideas down on paper. He's asked me to come over and

    a) add my two cents worth
    b) give him moral support
    c) throw a monkey wrench into the works
    d) give it to him straight

47. Look at those kids! Were we as impossible at their age? The boys stand on the street corner whistling at every pretty girl who goes by and the girls sit adoringly in the bleachers

    a) making eyes at their heroes
    b) carrying off the palm
    c) showing their true colors
    d) keeping tabs on everybody

48. I don't know what's happened to Sylvia. She's normally so down to earth and takes everything in her stride. But with his charm the new salesman at her office has really

    a) been in cahoots with her
    b) conjured up the devil
    c) added fuel to the flames
    d) swept her off her feet

49. The situation the refugees live in is really insupportable. They are forced to live without any dignity. It's time some of our politicians really

    a) went to bat for them
    b) hoist the white flag
    c) get out of line
    d) talked themselves hoarse

50. Maria was so unhappy. She felt herself completely spurned by men. Until somebody ... that it was her bad breath that was causing the problem. And then she did something about it!

    a) brought all his guns to bear on her
    b) talked her ear off
    c) shouted it from the roof-tops
    d) told her in a roundabout way

51. You'd better slow down on raiding the refrigerator for the best tidbits every night. Mom suspects it's you and she's

    a) hard on your heels
    b) laughing up her sleeve
    c) setting a precedent
    d) going to pay you back in kind

52. No, Maxine, you can't move in with Jeanie next semester, it's out of the question. You don't seem to realize that she lives in a luxury apartment. We just couldn't afford it. Please put it out of you mind; she has just

    a) killed two birds with one stone
    b) put a bug in your ear
    c) pulled the wool over your eyes
    d) beaten you to a pulp

53. You should have seen how calm Claire stayed throughout the meeting when everybody complained about how slow her department worked. At one point someone even came close to insulting her but, to my amazement, she just

    a) gave herself airs
    b) fell by the wayside
    c) let it pass
    d) kept a tight rein on them

54. What are the boys up to out in the backyard? It's awfully quiet out there. It's usually a sign that they're up to no good when they

    a) go into a huddle
    b) get in each other's hair
    c) blow their stack
    d) rack their brain

55. A cold front is due to move in, and fog is forecast for their destination airport, so I'd say if we don't give them clearance for take-off now, the flight will have to be postponed. If there are no objections,

    a) that's water over the dam
    b) I'll put a spoke in their wheel
    c) I'll give them the go-ahead
    d) that's the upshot of the matter

56. There's no way to accomplish anything at a family conference with Billy present. No matter what anyone says and regardless of how little he knows about a subject, he's always got to

    a) add his two cents worth
    b) put things on the shelf
    c) howl with the pack
    d) act on his own authority

57. Bryan simply hasn't got a mind of his own. It's really frustrating trying to get him to agree to anything, because he only listens to his brother. Whenever it comes to making a decision, he won't let reason be his guide. ...

    a) That's no bed of roses
    b) He'll make it by the skin of his teeth.
    c) He puts it into cold storage.
    d) He dances to his brother's tune!

58. Larry's a nice guy, but he keeps coming over for dinner and then just sits around the house. I think he's forgotten how I love to get out, even if it's only for a ride in the country. I think it's about time for me to

    a) give him a broad hint
    b) make eyes at him
    c) sweep him off his feet
    d) throw a monkey wrench into the works

59. Cheer up, Cindy, the world isn't coming to an end just because Bill has lost his job. He's an expert craftsman and will find another job with no trouble, believe me. Besides, we're here if you need help. ...

    a) It won't cost an arm and a leg.
    b) That's the upshot of the matter.
    c) Don't let it get you down.
    d) Let it pass.

60. Look, honey, I'm not really sure the kids want to go on vacation with us this summer. Perhaps they're just not saying anything so as not to hurt our feelings. Would you talk to them when you catch them at an opportune moment and sort of ... about it?

    a) bring things under one roof
    b) make both ends meet
    c) clear the air
    d) feel them out

61. It's a little too early to apply for the job, because the position hasn't been released yet, but as soon as it is, I'll be in touch. Don't worry, I'll watch what develops and

    a) won't let them get me down
    b) keep you up to date
    c) keep a stiff upper lip
    d) shout the news from the roof-tops

62. Your husband will be furious when he hears that you have taken on a part-time job again. He's not going to like the freedom that extra income will give you. He doesn't want to share decision-making with anyone, since he feels that he alone should

    a) put the cart before the horse
    b) have things handed to him on a silver platter
    c) live high off the hog
    d) rule the roost

63. If we could get a quick loan from Guarantee Trust, it would give us breathing room until we are solvent again, and meanwhile we could pay our overdue bills. That would

    a) not be worth a damn
    b) not cost an arm and a leg
    c) keep out creditors in check
    d) feather our nest

64. Look at the mess Mary's room is in. I can't stand it anymore. I'm going to confront her with it as soon as she gets home. There's got to be some way to

    a) lure her into a trap
    b) tell her in a roundabout way
    c) take her in
    d) make her shape up

65. You promised you'd do your homework regularly from now on, and now it turns out you are still not doing it. Starting today, you show me what you have done before you step outside this house. That is the only way I can

    a) keep a stiff upper lip
    b) talk your ear off
    c) wash my hands of it
    d) keep tabs on you

66. What's all this whispering? You know you won't be able to keep it a secret from me forever, whatever it is. So let's stop these little games and let's make an effort to

    a) pull the chestnuts out of the fire
    b) clear the air
    c) tread on delicate ground
    d) hoist up the white flag

67. That wine tastes decidedly watery. I bet it was Harry's doing. He's so tight with his money. I wonder if he really thinks that his guests won't

    a) see through his little game
    b) call the shots
    c) have his head
    d) let themselves in for it

68. I see less and less of Joe since he's gotten married. He says it's just because he has to study for his final exams, but I think it's his wife. If he goes out with the boys a lot, she can't

    a) throw dust in his eyes
    b) treat him with kid gloves
    c) keep a tight rein on him
    d) give it to him straight

69. All right, I won't try to hide the truth from you any longer. I don't want to give you a false sense of security, so I'm going to

    a) strike while the iron is hot
    b) give it to you straight
    c) hit the bull's-eye
    d) stick my neck out

70. Marvin thinks he can get away with anything he tries. Now he wants to buy that Session clock down in the secondhand store just so Herbert won't get it. Herbert's been saving up for it for weeks and Marvin doesn't really want it at all. I'm going to buy it first and then sell it to Herbert when he gets the money together.

    a) The tables are turned!
    b) That'll put a spoke in Marvin's wheel!
    c) That'll take the cake!
    d) That goes without saying!

71. Doggone it! Time goes by so fast. I was going to sign up for that real estate course down at the high school so I could earn some extra money, but now the deadline is past. Another golden opportunity

    a) happens only once in a blue moon
    b) has dropped out of sight
    c) is water under the bridge
    d) has slipped through my fingers

72. The mayor announced last night that he'd had about all he was going to take from the garbage men. It is clear that he has ... for failing to return to the negotiating table.

    a) been taken in by their leaders
    b) gone into a huddle with their leaders
    c) drawn a bead on their leaders
    d) moved heaven and earth with their leaders

73. He's a good student, but he should be even better. He just doesn't put in any effort. I think it's time I gave him something less than an A in order to

    a) put a bug in his ear
    b) bring all my guns to bear on him
    c) keep him in check
    d) throw a scare into him

74. I could kick myself. After all I've heard about door-to-door salesmen, I should have been smarter than to sign anything. I swear, though, this is the last time I'll

    a) bury my head in the sand
    b) walk into a salesman's trap
    c) put all my eggs in one basket
    d) rest on my oars

75. Have you heard about the latest neighborhood feud? That old biddy next door is so vindictive and mean, I swear

    a) she'd talk your ear off
    b) she'd put the cart before the horse
    c) she's in league with the devil
    d) she'll kick the bucket

76. I think it would be better if you don't mention to Andrea that Richard was in town. If she were to find out he was here without calling or seeing her, that would be sure to

    a) breed bad blood
    b) stink to high heaven
    c) happen only once in a blue moon
    d) hit the bull's-eye

77. That man down in the so-called antique shop on Main St. really ought to be run out of town. At first I thought he just didn't know enough about his business, but now that I've heard his sales pitch I'm convinced he simply enjoys

    a) handling people with kid gloves
    b) sailing under false colors
    c) feathering his nest
    d) taking people in

78. Billy told the bully down at the kindergarden yesterday that the next time he so much as touched his little sister, he'd

    a) not be worth a tinker's damn
    b) beat him to a pulp
    c) have a firm grip on him
    d) bury his head in the sand

79. Earl had been trying to outwit his colleague for months. When he finally got an inside tip about secret dealings the other man had with the underworld, that

    a) was the upshot of the matter
    b) stank to high heaven
    c) was no bed of roses
    d) was music to his ears

80. Be careful in your dealings with that land dealer. If you don't read the fine print in the contract and get an expert to look at the property before you buy, he's likely to

    a) build castles in Spain
    b) lure you into a trap
    c) hightail it out of there
    d) get it for a song

81. The walls in that new apartment complex are so thin that you feel you're right there in the middle of the fight every time the neighbors

    a) pull the chestnuts out of the fire
    b) put up a fierce resistance
    c) get into each other's hair
    d) start the ball rolling

82. Wow! Did Mrs. Brice ... at the fund-raising dinner last night. She went on and on about some idiot politician she'd heard speaking on the radio the day before, only to discover that he was sitting at the table across from her.

    a) put her foot in it
    b) give herself airs
    c) carry off the palm
    d) tilt at windmills

83. Marjorie's been looking for an excuse to ditch her husband for years. He doesn't realize it, but by taking up with his new secretary, he's

    a) playing right into his wife's hands
    b) building castles in the air
    c) adorning himself with borrowed plumes
    d) giving her a gentle hint

84. I've got to be really careful with my boss's new car. He made it pretty clear that if I got so much as a scratch on it, he'd

    a) beat his breast
    b) have my head
    c) paint the town red
    d) pull the wool over my eyes

85. I haven't forgotten that Wilbur went and told the boss on me when I lost an account last week. Just wait. The day will come when I'll be able to

    a) change my tune
    b) see through his racket
    c) add fuel to the flames
    d) pay him back in kind

86. Uncle Hubert came home from the fair with another useless gadget that cost him a lot of money. Somehow he can never resist a fast-talking salesman, and so whenever a wheeler-dealer delivers his sales pitch well, Uncle Hubert

    a) sees stars
    b) cashes in on it
    c) is taken in by him
    d) puts a spoke in his wheel

87. Harriet quickly withdrew from the business venture she'd been planning as soon as she realized that her partners lacked the necessary funds and were just trying to

    a) pull the wool over her eyes
    b) feel her out
    c) call the shots
    d) creep away with their tail between their legs

88. It's time someone thought about saving what's left of nature. I'm in favor of ... for the cause of protecting the trees and grass in our town.

    a) letting myself in
    b) swallowing the bitter pill
    c) clearing the air
    d) taking up arms

89. If you'd ride your bike to work, that would ... You'd be saving money and doing something for your health.

    a) kill two birds with one stone.
    b) be six of one and half-a-dozen of the other.
    c) add fuel to the flames.
    d) keep you up to date.

90. You needn't worry about Jonathan handling the business while we go on vacation. He ... the construction crew, so the work will get done well and on time.

    a) won't bat an eyelash with
    b) has a firm grip on
    c) will go to bat for
    d) will go into a huddle with

91. If we're all agreed that we'd rather spend our vacation in the mountains than at the seashore, we have a pretty good chance of persuading Father. We'll just have to

    a) make both ends meet
    b) give him moral support
    c) bring all our guns to bear on him
    d) build castles in the air

92. Even though both of us are working only part-time, between our two salaries there's just enough money coming in to

    a) be a godsend
    b) make ends meet
    c) play it safe
    d) save for a rainy day

93. The two teams have the same record going into the championship games. I wonder who's going to

    a) carry off the palm
    b) rule the roost
    c) be on the wrong track
    d) take the reins

94. Susan is a real friend. Countless times when the rest of us have gotten ourselves into difficulties, she's come to our rescue and

    a) made a mess of things
    b) treated us with kid gloves
    c) brought things under one roof
    d) pulled the chestnuts out of the fire

95. I'm really delighted with my new rocking chair. I spotted it at a garage sale last week and

    a) drew a bead on it
    b) didn't let anybody get me down
    c) got it for a song
    d) it was music to my ears

96. There's nothing more difficult than getting people to open their purses and donate money to a cause. What do you think of the idea of holding a bazaar to

   a) hoist up the white flag?
   b) be the talk of the town?
   c) give them the go-ahead?
   d) start the ball rolling?

97. The traffic chaos downtown is really unbearable. I think our city council should finally ... and implement the park-and-ride plan.

   a) have something up its sleeve
   b) let it pass
   c) dance to someone else's tune
   d) take the bull by the horns

98. I hadn't known Jack was a collector of wooden toys. It was a lucky choice when I gave him a rocking horse for his birthday. I really

   a) took the bull by the horns
   b) called the shots
   c) hit the bull's-eye
   d) flew off the handle

99. A specimen like this doesn't become available very often. I can't begin to guess when we'll have another one to offer you. You'd better

   a) not mince words
   b) give it to me straight
   c) stick your neck out
   d) strike while the iron is hot

100. With her new job and the better pay, Patty is finally in a position to repay her debts, get a few new items for her apartment and

   a) save something for a rainy day
   b) be in league with the Joneses
   c) laugh up her sleeve
   d) not make a big issue of things

101. Ever since the boss retired and his son took over, this outfit has been going downhill. He's going to manage us into bankruptcy. I think it's time we made it clear to him that somebody else ought to

   a) take the helm
   b) be a godsend
   c) play it safe
   d) smell a rat

102. Karen has really done well with her photography. Ever since she had her one-woman show at the gallery in New York, she has honors

   a) going full blast
   b) handed to her on a silver platter
   c) spreading like wildfire
   d) slipping through her fingers

103. We can get an initial injunction against the atomic energy plant they want to build in our county if we file a petition with at least 5000 signatures. But we need them by next Friday. We'll really have to ... and we need all the help we can get.

   a) live high off the hog
   b) burn our bridges
   c) ram our heads against a wall
   d) put our shoulders to the wheel

104. If our team wins the championship this weekend, there's going to be a fantastic celebration. We'll round up all our friends and

   a) paint the town red
   b) go down the drain
   c) call the tune
   d) throw dust in everybody's eyes

105. Curt has a real solid head for business. I don't know how he manages to do it, but every time there's a money-making proposition in this town, he's there to

   a) be taken in by someone
   b) cash in on it
   c) kill two birds with one stone
   d) stand his ground

106. I guess they're not going to be able to remove Ms. Kaydee from the P.T.A. board. By now she ... and it would take an act of Congress to get rid of her.

   a) has smelled a rat
   b) has adorned herself with borrowed plumes
   c) is on the skids
   d) is securely in the driver's seat

107. I don't care what the landlord says about proper ventilation and the like. What's wrong with our apartment is the result of faulty construction. It's up to him to fix it and I intend to ... at next week's meeting.

   a) measure everything with the same yardstick
   b) put a bug in somebody's ear
   c) make it by the skin of my teeth
   d) stand my ground

108. Erik wants very much to spend a year going to school in America and he's prepared to ... to make it possible.

   a) throw a monkey wrench into the works
   b) beat his breast
   c) have someone's head
   d) move heaven and earth

109. I think Jonie has earned a break. After all, you must admit that she has worked very hard lately, so if she wants to take some time off, that's fine with me. And don't scold her for coming home late. I think it would be best not to

   a) let it get us down
   b) make a big issue of it
   c) harm a hair on her head
   d) strike while the iron is hot

110. There is no longer any doubt that something has gone wrong in our dealings with that company. They don't respond to our letters, and they haven't paid a single bill since January. Am I the only one to

   a) smell a rat?
   b) see stars?
   c) breed bad blood?
   d) have something up my sleeve?

111. Let's make it clear to the minister that his country must develop fiscal responsibility before we commit ourselves to further development loans. But it's important to broach the subject to him very carefully, because we are

   a) making it by the skin of our teeth
   b) treading on delicate ground
   c) talking ourselves hoarse
   d) not making a big fuss about it

112. Gosh, I haven't seen Charlie in ages. Do you think he's still working on his book? For all practical purposes,

   a) that is water over the dam
   b) it's the talk of the town
   c) he's dropped out of sight
   d) he's making no bones about it

113. Boy, did I get told off by Amelia today. She didn't even try to hide her dislike, I can tell you. She considered me an intruder at the picnic and

   a) took me in
   b) made no bones about it
   c) gave me a broad hint
   d) went to bat for me

114. Time to bathe Rover again. I dread the struggle every single time. That beast always knows when the time for another bout with soap and water is approaching. So he runs and hides, and when you try to pull him out from under the bed,

   a) he puts up a fierce resistance
   b) the tables are turned
   c) he makes eyes at you
   d) he goes full blast

115. It's about time for us to get our tax refund. It's been months since we filed our return. They want their money right away when there's a balance due, but whenever there's a refund, they find a way to

   a) have a firm grip on it
   b) put it on the shelf
   c) pay you back in kind
   d) save it for a rainy day

116. Tonight everybody and his brother is going to be on the roads because of the long holiday weekend, so be really careful driving, and whatever you do please

   a) be on your guard against the other drivers
   b) don't harm a hair on anybody's head
   c) be securely in the driver's seat
   d) take your life into your hands

117. There have been so many conflicting reports about a devaluation that we should try to get an official statement. Even if the government hedges on it, we may find out enough to

   a) grab the bull by the horns
   b) go down the drain
   c) see how the land lies
   d) rack our brain

118. You can count Father out. He's tried to talk sense into his sister for years, but now that she has gone and invested every cent she has in that shady land deal in Florida, he's given up on her. And as to her financial dealings,

   a) he's washing his hands of them
   b) the tables are turned
   c) it's six of one and half-a-dozen of the other
   d) they're getting out of line

119. Wish me luck. Today I have my little talk with the boss about my future in the company. I've tried to delay that meeting long enough. Much as I hate it, I've got to

   a) set a precedent
   b) act on my own authority
   c) be in league with him
   d) venture into the lion's den

120. The Friedman plan doesn't seem to have the desired effect on the economy. We should be thinking of alternatives. If the plan doesn't take hold by the first of the year, it'll have to

   a) be put into cold storage
   b) fall by the wayside
   c) be touch and go
   d) sail under false colors

121. Now that both of his folks have died, he's sold that last parcel of land, too. I bet he won't even come back to visit. He's

   a) made a mess of things
   b) crept away with his tail between his legs
   c) burned his bridges behind him
   d) hightailed it out of here

122. We have all our figures together, but the problem will be to satisfy each of the individual parties involved. Somehow we must arrive at an equitable solution in such a manner that all factions are

   a) put into cold storage
   b) living high off the hog
   c) brought under one roof
   d) having things handed to them on a silver platter

123. Those AD&D stocks I inherited will make us rich yet. I'm telling you confidentially that there will be another three-way split of the shares, but

   a) it goes without saying
   b) it's touch and go
   c) I'm weighing my words
   d) don't shout it from the roof-tops

124. It might be a good idea to diversify our holdings and not sink all our profits into just one enterprise. It just doesn't pay to

   a) pull the wool over everybody's eyes
   b) draw a bead on one company
   c) keep a tight rein on things
   d) put all one's eggs in one basket

125. The city is strapped for money, and I understand if they want to curtail snow removal and stop servicing the city picnic grounds and stuff like that, but they are threatening to close the schools now, too. We have to have some priorities! It simply won't do to

   a) happen only once in a blue moon
   b) measure everything with the same yardstick
   c) be on the skids
   d) be taken in by them

126. Andy's dented the fender on David's car. He feels really bad about it, and has been worrying all week about telling him. David's coming back from his vacation tonight, so it won't be long now before Andy has got to

   a) make himself scarce
   b) swallow the bitter pill
   c) put a spoke in his wheel
   d) blow his stack

127. Well, let's get to work and tackle all this dirt and grime. It won't go away regardless of how long we ... It's time we did something about it.

   a) measure everything with the same yardstick.
   b) make ourselves scarce.
   c) put our shoulders to the wheel.
   d) bury our heads in the sand.

128. Oh, I wish I could live the last week over again. I tried so hard to make things right for everybody, but all I managed to do was

   a) talk myself hoarse
   b) make a mess of things
   c) throw dust in people's eyes
   d) put things into cold storage

129. Willy wanted to show his mom that he could mow the lawn all by himself. But when all he managed to do was break the lawnmower and slice a sizable chunk out of the front yard, he

   a) ended up on the rocks
   b) crept away with his tail between his legs
   c) dropped out of sight
   d) threw a scare into her

130. Mother is such a crusading spirit, I wish she'd invest her energies in causes that stand a chance of succeeding. It's a real shame that instead she constantly goes about

   a) putting a bug in people's ears
   b) adorning herself with borrowed plumes
   c) tilting at windmills
   d) giving herself airs

131. You'd better beware. I'm for giving everybody a chance, but Winston is such a lazy good-for-nothing that if you hired him, you'd really be

   a) walking into his trap
   b) calling the tune
   c) hard on his heels
   d) letting yourself in for something

132. You've been trying for months to keep this little newspaper going, but the big dailies are winning over more and more of your advertisers. I'm afraid before long you'll have to ... and sell out.

   a) hoist the white flag
   b) start the ball rolling
   c) take the reins
   d) throw a scare into them

133. Millie and the boys have been whispering all morning, and whenever I walk by their desks everything suddenly goes quiet. I know they .... I just wish I knew what it is.

   a) are on their guard against something
   b) have something up their sleeve
   c) are racking their brains about something
   d) are taking up arms for something

134. Oh, what a mess there is on this desk. I know that announcement arrived before we went on vacation. But if you think I can find it among all this accumulated mail in the five minutes before we have to leave

   a) you are on the wrong track
   b) it's certainly no bed of roses
   c) it'll dawn on me
   d) I'll lend you a helping hand

135. It's no use. You know Father. When he does things, he does them thoroughly. If you try to talk him out of driving up for your graduation, you'll just

   a) throw in the towel
   b) give him a broad hint
   c) run into a brick wall
   d) be taking your life into your hands

136. Whatever you do, don't tell Frank what Judy said about him. He's mad at her already and you'd only be

   a) adding fuel to the flames
   b) sticking up for her
   c) giving him the go-ahead
   d) luring him into a trap

137. I'm not surprised that Mr. Fry has retired to a cozy estate in Florida. He's been ... at the expense of his partners for years and can afford to live in grand style now, of course.

   a) putting matters on the shelf
   b) weighing his words
   c) feathering his nest
   d) lending everybody a helping hand

138. Nothing is going to go wrong. Now, please, for once let's set out on our vacation cheerfully and with a positive attitude. Although there are always things that could go wrong, you needn't be so pessimistic and ..., especially when everything is going so smoothly.

    a) have my head
    b) conjure up the devil
    c) go on the warpath
    d) move heaven and earth

139. It seems as though the backers of that new highway are gaining more and more supporters. We've got to find some way to stop them soon. If there was only some way we could

    a) throw a monkey wrench into the works!
    b) be on our guard against them!
    c) be securely in the driver's seat!
    d) blow our stack!

140. Bert's father is willing to set him up in business, but Bert is a stubborn kid and insists on trying to work his way up from the bottom. At the moment it looks as if he's ..., but maybe he'll succeed.

    a) getting something for a song
    b) walking into someone's trap
    c) ramming his head against a wall
    d) ruling the roost

141. Why can't you ever take care of things one step at a time? With your constant impatience, you try to get ahead in leaps and bounds and inevitably wind up

    a) getting into each other's hair
    b) going on the warpath
    c) hightailing it out of there
    d) putting the cart before the horse

142. You've always been so lax about taking care of your teeth. Despite the dentist's warnings and common sense you kept eating sweets and forgetting to brush. Now you have to spend months and thousands on dental treatment.

    a) That's the upshot of the matter.
    b) You'd better change your tune.
    c) You've ended up on the rocks.
    d) You'll be howling with the pack.

143. Uncle Arthur came home from the hospital today looking cheerful and ready to take on the world again. It is amazing how quickly he recovered from his operation when you think that only two weeks ago the doctor said

    a) he was treading on delicate ground
    b) he would wash his hands of the matter
    c) he was taking his life in his hands
    d) it was touch and go

144. The Board of Health insists that we all go and get a flu shot. When the swimming team brought back the Asian flu, ... Now half the town is sick.

    a) it spread like wildfire
    b) it swept people off their feet
    c) we put up a fierce resistance
    d) we ended up on the rocks

145. Last semester Harvey was carrying a class load of 19 credits, working four hours a day delivering bread in the wee hours of the morning, and taking care of his baby sister during the afternoons. That was certainly

   a) no bed of roses
   b) striking while the iron is hot
   c) music to his ears
   d) swallowing the bitter pill

146. James needs money to finance his father's hospital bills. He's used up all of his savings and will have to get a loan. If he goes to a bank, ... he'll have to put up some collateral. The best idea would probably be to mortgage the house.

   a) it goes without saying that
   b) they'll tell him in a roundabout way that
   c) it will dawn on him that
   d) they'll keep a tight rein on him

147. That computer outfit called again and has asked us to schedule a meeting for tomorrow afternoon. I have a feeling they're getting nervous. We'd better have the contract typed and ready for signing on the spot or our project may

   a) fall by the wayside
   b) get out of line
   c) go down the drain
   d) be on the skids

148. We've simply got to keep next weekend free for the big game, even if we don't follow sports that religiously. Our high-school team has reached the national championships, and something like that

   a) goes without saying
   b) really moves heaven and earth
   c) happens only once in a blue moon
   d) paints the town red

149. You make the decision. I simply don't care whether we spend our vacation in Spain or in Italy. As far as I'm concerned,

   a) it kills two birds with one stone
   b) it's six of one and half-a-dozen of the other
   c) we can rest on our oars
   d) the tables are turned

150. These days Billy can't talk about anything but that photography course he's dying to take. I guess we'll let him attend. Since it's part of the after-school program, I'm pretty sure

   a) he'll see how the land lies
   b) he'll venture into the lion's den
   c) he won't be on the wrong track
   d) it won't cost an arm and a leg

151. There's an ad in the newspaper offering adventure and fantastic pay for summer work abroad. You have to be young, pretty, with a good figure, and unattached. It's guaranteed not to be a sales position. That sort of thing

   a) keeps you up to date!
   b) beats you to a pulp!
   c) sweeps you off your feet!
   d) stinks to high heaven!

152. They told me their apartment was much too expensive for them. They begged me to come and look at it in the hope that I would take it off their hands. After I had decided to rent it and had already consulted an interior decorator about the redecorations, they suddenly changed their minds about moving out.

    a) Did they put a bug in my ear!
    b) If that doesn't take the cake!
    c) They've shown their true colors.
    d) Did I see stars!

153. There's a press conference today that I must go to in order to be able to write my story and not run the danger of losing my job. Herbert is at work and can't get away. The children are both sick in bed and the baby sitter's out of town. Oh, Aunt Mary, ... I don't know what I'd have done if you hadn't come to stay with the children.

    a) you are sticking up for me
    b) you're a godsend
    c) give me moral support
    d) lend me a helping hand

154. Philip worked in his study all afternoon, muttering in exasperation at frequent intervals. When he came out for dinner, we asked what had upset him so. "Every time I was going along smoothly with my drawing, the point on my new drafting pencil would break," he said. "This new-fangled stuff

    a) is not worth a damn."
    b) takes the cake."
    c) slips through your fingers."
    d) carries off the palm."

155. It's hard to believe that you haven't heard of Mr. Wyatt's appointment to the school board.

    a) Nobody made any bones about it.
    b) It's the talk of the town.
    c) He really ran into a brick wall.
    d) I think they've conjured up the devil.

156. There was a time when Stephanie and I couldn't stand each other. Her impatience drove me to distraction and she couldn't tolerate my chattiness. Since then we've come a long way. We both work with handicapped people and while she's learned to be more patient, I've learned to listen to others. In the course of the years we've become good friends and our earlier differences

    a) have bred bad blood
    b) have slipped through our fingers
    c) have been put on the shelf
    d) are water over the dam

157. The school refuses to excuse students from classes just before or just after a vacation. They are afraid that even one case would ... and that pretty soon everybody would be extending their vacation time.

    a) set a precedent
    b) give them to go-ahead
    c) put the cart before the horse
    d) pull the wool over our eyes

158. It used to be that I took my daughter by the hand, took her places, explained things to her. Now that she's almost grown and has learned many things that I know nothing about, ... She teaches me.

    a) she keeps me in check
    b) she keeps close tabs on me
    c) she plays into my hand
    d) the tables are turned

ANSWER KEY - *Exercises*

UNIT 1

TEST YOURSELF:

1 b, 2 d, 3 d, 4 c, 5 c, 6 a, 7 d, 8 a, 9 c, 10 c, 11 a, 12 b, 13 c, 14 d, 15 a, 16 b, 17 d, 18 b, 19 a, 20 b, 21 d, 22 a

RECOGNITION:

1 f, 2 d, 3 e, 4 a, 5 c, 6 d, 7 b, 8 f, 9 c, 10 f, 11 e, 12 b, 13 b, 14 c, 15 b, 16 c, 17 c, 18 a, 19 a, 20 c, 21 d, 22 c

STORY COMPLETION:

mince words
calling the shots
show their true colors
acted on their own authority
live high off the hog
rest on their oars
made it by the skin of his teeth
take his life into his hands
stuck his neck out
hightail it out of there
racking their brains

it dawned on them
build castles in the air
batting an eyelash
put a brave face on it
play it safe
kept a stiff upper lip
made himself scarce
called the tune
change his tune
going full blast
weighing his words

SITUATION FIT:

1. putting a brave face on it
2. racking my brain
3. weigh your words
4. calls the shots
5. taking my life into my hands
6. living high off the hog
7. keep a stiff upper lip
8. building castles in the air
9. mince words
10. hightail it out of here
11. play it safe
12. changed his tune
13. stick your neck out
14. go full blast
15. show his true colors
16. it dawned on you
17. made themselves scarce
18. acting on his own authority
19. made it by the skin of my teeth
20. bat an eyelash
21. rest on your oars
22. calls the tune

UNIT 2

TEST YOURSELF:

1 b, 2 a, 3 d, 4 b, 5 b, 6 a, 7 d, 8 b, 9 b, 10 a, 11 c, 12 c, 13 d, 14 a, 15 b, 16 c, 17 c, 18 d

RECOGNITION:

1 c, 2 b, 3 d, 4 f, 5 f, 6 a, 7 d, 8 e, 9 d, 10 d, 11 b, 12 c, 13 c, 14 a, 15 a, 16 d, 17 c, 18 c

STORY COMPLETION:

saw stars
talk yourself hoarse
beat your breast
laugh up his sleeve
adorn yourself with borrowed
 plumes
sail under false colors
throw in the towel
blew your stack
kick the bucket

flew off the handle
talked his ear off
go on the warpath
be on the skids
got out of line
giving yourself airs
end up on the rocks
fall by the wayside
howl with the pack

SITUATION FIT:

1. sailing under false colors
2. kicked the bucket
3. talk your ear off
4. adorning himself with
   borrowed plumes
5. getting out of line
6. go on the warpath
7. end up on the rocks
8. beating your breast
9. fall by the wayside
10. blow my stack
11. laughing up her sleeve
12. is on the skids
13. talk myself hoarse
14. howls with the pack
15. throw in the towel
16. give yourself airs
17. fly off the handle
18. saw stars

UNIT 3

TEST YOURSELF:

1 a, 2 c, 3 b, 4 d, 5 a, 6 b, 7 d, 8 a, 9 c, 10 c

RECOGNITION:

1 c, 2 a, 3 d, 4 d, 5 a, 6 b, 7 d, 8 d, 9 a, 10 d

STORY COMPLETION:

lending ... a helping hand
making eyes at her
break it to you gently
throw dust in my eyes
treating you with kid gloves

harm a hair on anybody's head
sweep ... off their feet
go to bat for you
give you moral support
stick up for you

SITUATION FIT:

1. treat him with kid gloves
2. go to bat for me
3. lend him a helping hand
4. stick up for you
5. break it to me gently
6. sweep you off your feet
7. make eyes at
8. throw dust in my eyes
9. not harm a hair on anybody's head
10. giving me moral support

UNIT 4

TEST YOURSELF:

1 c, 2 b, 3 a, 4 a, 5 d, 6 d, 7 b, 8 d, 9 a, 10 c, 11 b, 12 c, 13 a, 14 d,
15 b, 16 a, 17 c, 18 d, 19 d

RECOGNITION:

1 c, 2 f, 3 b, 4 d, 5 f, 6 c, 7 b, 8 e, 9 e, 10 d, 11 b, 12 c, 13 b, 14 c,
15 c, 16 c, 17 a, 18 b, 19 c

STORY COMPLETION:

let it pass
hard on your heels
keep close tabs on
putting a bug in your ear
rule the roost
keep a tight rein on
go into a huddle
keep you up to date
given me the go-ahead
dance to my tune

keep you in check
see through your little game
put in your 2 cents worth
clear the air
let ... get you down
makes you shape up
given it to you straight from the shoulder
given a broad hint
feel me out

SITUATION FIT:

1. keep close tabs on him
2. make him shape up
3. rule the roost
4. keep him/her up to date
5. let it pass
6. add your 2 cents worth
7. going into a huddle
8. put a bug in her ear
9. keep a tight rein on him
10. give us a broad hint
11. keep ... in check
12. given me the go-ahead
13. hard on the heels
14. clear the air
15. see through his little game
16. dances to ... tune
17. don't let it get you down
18. feel her out
19. give it to him straight

UNIT 5

TEST YOURSELF:

1 b, 2 c, 3 a, 4 d, 5 a, 6 c, 7 b, 8 c, 9 a, 10 a, 11 c, 12 b, 13 a, 14 c, 15 d, 16 b, 17 c, 18 a

RECOGNITION:

1 a, 2 d, 3 a, 4 c, 5 c, 6 b, 7 a, 8 a, 9 d, 10 c, 11 b, 12 f, 13 g, 14 c, 15 c, 16 f, 17 e, 18 h

STORY COMPLETION:

put a spoke in our wheel
causes bad blood
throw a scare into them
are in cahoots with each other
walk into their trap
luring them into a trap
put their foot in it
be music to their ears
get into each other's hair
beat to a pulp ... you
playing into the hands of
have his head
draw a bead on us
take them in
slip through your fingers
be taken in by them
pull the wool over your eyes
pay them back in kind

SITUATION FIT:

1. in cahoots with them
2. took me in
3. breed bad blood
4. pay him back in kind
5. pull the wool over my eyes
6. throw a scare into her
7. beat you to a pulp
8. put your foot in it
9. be taken in by
10. put a spoke in his wheel
11. have his head
12. slip through our fingers
13. are in each other's hair
14. walking into his trap
15. play into our hands
16. drawing a bead on me
17. been music to your ears
18. lure someone into a trap

UNIT 6

TEST YOURSELF:

1 a, 2 b, 3 c, 4 d, 5 c, 6 a, 7 d, 8 d, 9 a, 10 c, 11 a, 12 d, 13 c, 14 a, 15 b, 16 b, 17 a, 18 c, 19 b, 20 c, 21 a

RECOGNITION:

1 c, 2 b, 3 h, 4 e, 5 b, 6 e, 7 g, 8 h, 9 d, 10 c, 11 a, 12 e, 13 d, 14 a, 15 b, 16 c, 17 c, 18 c, 19 c, 20 b, 21 c

STORY COMPLETION:

taken up arms for
got for a song
making ends meet
kill two birds with one stone
strike while the iron is hot
bring all your guns to bear on
had a firm grip on
move heaven and earth
stand my ground
saved for a rainy day
cash in on them

pull the chestnuts out of the fire
paint the town red
carry off the palm
start the ball rolling
is ... securely in the driver's seat
have ... handed to them on a silver
   platter
hit the bull's-eye
take the bull by the horns
put their shoulders to the wheel
take the helm

SITUATION FIT:

1. take the bull by the horns
2. making both ends meet
3. cashing in on
4. have a firm grip on
5. taken the reins
6. take up arms for
7. saving it for a rainy day
8. securely in the driver's
   seat
9. moved heaven and earth
10. got them for a song
11. put my shoulder to the wheel
12. strike while the iron is hot
13. pull the chestnuts out of the fire
14. hit the bull's-eye
15. kill two birds with one stone
16. bring all their guns to bear on
17. start the ball rolling
18. painted the town red
19. stand my ground
20. carry off the palm
21. handed to you on a silver
    platter

UNIT 7

TEST YOURSELF:

1 a, 2 a, 3 d, 4 b, 5 c, 6 b, 7 a, 8 c, 9 c, 10 b, 11 c, 12 b, 13 a, 14 c, 15 a, 16 c, 17 b

RECOGNITION:

1 a, 2 c, 3 d, 4 a, 5 b, 6 d, 7 c, 8 a, 9 d, 10 a, 11 a, 12 c, 13 c, 14 c, 15 g, 16 e, 17 a

STORY COMPLETION:

make a big issue of
put ... on the shelf
dropping out of sight
burn your bridges behind you
see how the land lies
putting ... in cold storage
tread on delicate ground
smell a rat
shouting ... from the roof-tops

wash our hands of it
put up a fierce resistance
make no bones about
venture into the lion's den
bring ... under one roof
on our guard against
measure everything with the same yardstick
putting all your eggs in one basket

SITUATION FIT:

1. burn my bridges behind me
2. bring ... under one roof
3. put it into cold storage
4. measure everything with the same yardstick
5. dropped out of sight
6. be on your guard against
7. treading on delicate ground
8. make no bones about
9. doesn't make a big issue of
10. see how the land lies
11. put all one's eggs in one basket
12. put it on the shelf
13. washed his hands of it
14. smell a rat
15. venture into the lion's den
16. shouting it from the roof-tops
17. put up a fierce resistance

UNIT 8

TEST YOURSELF:

1 a, 2 b, 3 c, 4 d, 5 c, 6 c, 7 d, 8 a, 9 c, 10 b, 11 a, 12 d, 13 b, 14 d, 15 c, 16 a

RECOGNITION:

1 c, 2 a, 3 f, 4 d, 5 c, 6 f, 7 e, 8 a, 9 a, 10 c, 11 d, 12 a, 13 d, 14 b, 15 c, 16 c

STORY COMPLETION:

swallow the bitter pill
be letting myself in for
running into a brick wall
are on the wrong track
ramming your head against a wall
hiding your head in the sand
mess you'll make of things
adding fuel to the flames
putting the cart before the horse
creep away with your tail between your legs
throw a monkey wrench into the works
feather my nest
have something up your sleeve
run up the white flag
conjure up the devil
tilting at windmills

SITUATION FIT:

1. throw a monkey wrench into the works
2. swallow the bitter pill
3. ram his head against a wall
4. crept away with his tail between his legs
5. add fuel to the flames
6. tilting at windmills
7. feather his nest
8. let yourself in for
9. bury your head in the sand
10. on the wrong track
11. have something up their sleeve
12. putting the cart before the horse
13. running into a brick wall
14. conjure up the devil
15. make a mess of things
16. run up the white flag

UNIT 9

TEST YOURSELF:

1 b, 2 a, 3 c, 4 a, 5 d, 6 a, 7 d, 8 d, 9 a, 10 b, 11 c, 12 d, 13 a, 14 b, 15 b, 16 a, 17 c

RECOGNITION:

1 g, 2 e, 3 a, 4 d, 5 b, 6 c, 7 b, 8 a, 9 f, 10 a, 11 d, 12 b, 13 c, 14 d, 15 c, 16 a, 17 b

STORY COMPLETION:

go down the drain
the tables are turned
that's the upshot of the matter
take the cake
it's ... a godsend
that is water over the dam
goes without saying
worth a damn
stink to high heaven
be no bed of roses
it's six of one and half-a-dozen of the other
It happens only once in a blue moon
touch and go
set a precedent
it will be the talk of the town
won't cost an arm and a leg
spread like wildfire

SITUATION FIT:

1. the tables are turned
2. aren't worth a tinker's damn
3. go down the drain
4. stinks to high heaven
5. happens only once in a blue moon
6. takes the cake
7. set a precedent
8. spreads like wildfire
9. it's six of one and half-a-dozen of the other
10. the upshot of the matter
11. won't cost an arm and a leg
12. it's the talk of the town
13. no bed of roses
14. be touch and go
15. That is water over the dam
16. is a godsend
17. It goes without saying

ANSWER KEY - Final Check

	a	b	c	d
1	2.15	*1.2*	6.19	4.13
2	2.5	6.16	*1.5*	8.6
3	4.13	9.14	*1.9*	3.8
4	2.11	*1.7*	1.18	5.13
5	6.15	6.20	*1.11*	2.9
6	*1.14*	4.12	7.17	6.9
7	2.2	3.9	*1.15*	5.11
8	2.10	*1.18*	8.10	8.7
9	*1.19*	8.13	3.7	8.2
10	9.5	6.7	7.13	*1.22*
11	6.17	1.10	*1.20*	1.15
12	*1.8*	2.13	9.8	9.13
13	5.3	4.14	5.8	*1.12*
14	9.17	8.4	4.16	*1.21*
15	2.7	3.6	7.12	*1.1*
16	1.14	7.9	4.7	*1.6*
17	*1.3*	3.10	8.16	2.4
18	8.12	*1.13*	6.2	6.8
19	6.11	6.21	5.7	*1.17*
20	6.11	*1.16*	5.18	4.10
21	5.14	6.9	*1.4*	7.14
22	2.10	*1.10*	1.21	8.16
23	*2.18*	9.11	7.16	7.17
24	7.4	7.10	7.13	*2.17*
25	1.2	1.6	1.8	*2.5*
26	5.2	*2.2*	8.9	2.9
27	1.9	*2.7*	1.15	4.1
28	*2.13*	1.3	1.20	7.4
29	*2.10*	1.19	8.1	1.16
30	7.7	4.5	*2.12*	7.5
31	4.10	6.20	*2.15*	1.17
32	*2.1*	5.11	4.2	5.7
33	1.12	4.16	*2.3*	7.8

	a	b	c	d
34	4.2	1.22	*2.6*	1.1
35	*2.16*	9.4	9.15	8.3
36	7.3	*2.9*	7.11	9.1
37	6.18	8.5	*2.8*	8.15
38	2.6	*2.14*	6.10	8.3
39	5.7	5.9	6.13	*2.11*
40	*2.4*	6.14	4.18	2.18
41	4.8	7.5	*3.1*	6.1
42	4.3	1.15	4.19	*3.10*
43	1.14	*3.6*	7.1	2.7
44	4.11	7.15	*3.5*	6.12
45	8.5	*3.4*	6.3	1.4
46	4.13	*3.9*	8.11	4.17
47	*3.2*	6.14	1.3	4.3
48	5.4	8.15	8.8	*3.7*
49	*3.8*	8.14	2.14	2.1
50	6.6	2.12	7.9	*3.3*
51	*4.2*	2.4	9.14	5.18
52	6.4	*4.4*	5.17	5.10
53	2.15	2.17	*4.1*	4.6
54	*4.7*	5.9	2.8	1.10
55	9.6	5.1	*4.9*	9.3
56	*4.13*	7.2	2.18	1.4
57	9.10	1.7	7.6	*4.10*
58	*4.18*	3.2	3.7	8.11
59	9.16	9.3	*4.15*	4.1
60	7.14	6.3	4.14	*4.19*
61	4.15	*4.8*	1.17	7.9
62	8.9	6.17	1.5	*4.5*
63	9.8	9.16	*4.11*	8.12
64	5.6	3.3	5.14	*4.16*
65	1.17	2.12	7.10	*4.3*
66	6.12	*4.14*	7.7	8.14

	a	b	c	d		a	b	c	d
67	*4.12*	1.2	5.12	8.2	103	1.5	7.4	8.5	*6.20*
68	3.4	3.5	*4.6*	4.17	104	*6.13*	9.1	1.19	3.4
69	6.5	*4.17*	6.18	1.9	105	5.16	*6.11*	6.4	6.9
70	9.2	*5.1*	9.4	9.7	106	7.8	2.5	2.13	*6.16*
71	9.12	7.3	9.6	*5.15*	107	7.16	4.4	1.7	*6.9*
72	5.16	4.7	*5.13*	6.8	108	8.11	2.2	5.12	*6.8*
73	4.4	6.6	4.11	*5.3*	109	4.15	*7.1*	3.6	6.5
74	8.6	*5.5*	7.17	1.6	110	*7.8*	2.3	5.2	8.13
75	2.12	8.9	*5.4*	2.9	111	1.7	*7.7*	2.1	7.1
76	*5.2*	9.9	9.12	6.18	112	9.6	9.15	*7.3*	7.12
77	3.5	2.6	8.12	*5.14*	113	5.14	*7.12*	4.18	3.8
78	9.8	*5.10*	6.7	8.6	114	*7.11*	9.2	3.2	1.21
79	9.3	9.9	9.10	*5.8*	115	6.7	*7.2*	5.18	6.10
80	1.13	*5.6*	1.11	6.2	116	*7.15*	3.6	6.16	1.8
81	6.12	7.11	*5.9*	6.15	117	6.19	9.1	*7.5*	1.10
82	*5.7*	2.15	6.14	8.16	118	*7.10*	9.2	9.11	2.14
83	*5.11*	1.13	2.5	3.3	119	9.14	1.4	5.4	*7.13*
84	2.2	*5.12*	6.13	5.17	120	*7.6*	2.17	9.13	2.6
85	1.20	4.12	8.8	*5.18*	121	8.7	8.10	*7.4*	1.11
86	2.3	6.11	*5.16*	5.1	122	7.6	1.5	*7.14*	6.17
87	*5.17*	4.19	1.2	8.10	123	9.7	9.13	1.22	*7.9*
88	8.2	8.1	4.14	*6.1*	124	5.17	5.13	4.6	*7.17*
89	*6.4*	9.11	8.8	4.8	125	9.12	*7.16*	2.13	5.16
90	1.14	*6.7*	3.8	4.7	126	1.18	*8.1*	5.1	2.8
91	6.3	3.9	*6.6*	1.13	127	7.16	1.18	6.20	*8.6*
92	9.5	*6.3*	1.16	6.10	128	2.1	*8.7*	3.4	7.6
93	*6.14*	4.5	8.4	6.21	129	2.16	*8.10*	7.3	5.3
94	8.7	3.5	7.14	*6.12*	130	4.4	2.5	*8.16*	2.15
95	5.13	4.15	*6.2*	5.8	131	5.5	1.19	4.2	*8.2*
96	8.14	9.15	4.9	*6.15*	132	*8.14*	6.15	6.21	5.3
97	8.13	4.1	4.10	*6.19*	133	7.15	*8.13*	1.10	6.1
98	6.19	1.2	*6.18*	2.10	134	*8.4*	9.10	1.12	3.1
99	1.1	4.17	1.9	*6.5*	135	2.7	4.18	*8.3*	1.8
100	*6.10*	5.4	2.4	7.1	136	*8.8*	3.10	4.9	5.6
101	*6.21*	9.5	1.16	7.8	137	7.2	1.22	*8.12*	3.1
102	1.21	*6.17*	9.17	5.15	138	5.12	*8.15*	2.11	6.8

	a	b	c	d
139	*8.11*	7.15	6.16	2.8
140	6.2	5.5	*8.5*	4.5
141	5.9	2.11	1.11	*8.9*
142	*9.3*	1.20	2.16	2.18
143	7.7	7.10	1.8	*9.13*
144	*9.17*	3.7	7.11	2.16
145	*9.10*	6.5	5.8	8.1
146	*9.7*	3.3	1.12	4.6
147	2.17	2.14	*9.1*	2.13
148	9.7	6.8	*9.12*	6.13
149	6.4	*9.11*	1.6	9.2
150	7.5	7.13	8.4	*9.16*
151	4.8	5.10	3.7	*9.9*
152	4.4	*9.4*	1.3	2.3
153	3.10	*9.5*	3.9	3.1
154	*9.8*	9.4	5.15	6.14
155	7.12	*9.15*	8.3	8.15
156	5.2	5.15	7.2	*9.6*
157	*9.14*	4.9	8.9	5.17
158	4.11	4.3	5.11	*9.2*

ENGLISH INDEX

* = idiom entry

A
vanish into thin **air** 7.3
*clear the **air** 4.14
*give oneself **airs** 2.15
s.t. won't cost an* **arm *and a leg* 9.16
lay down one's **arms** 8.14
take up **arms** *for s.t.* 6.1
act on one's own* **authority 1.4
give s.o. the **ax** 5.12

B
put one's **back** *to it* 6.20
start/get the* **ball *rolling* 6.15
*go to **bat** *for s.o.* *3.8, 6.1
***be** *taken in by s.o.* 5.14, *5.16
*draw a **bead** *on s.o.* 5.13
beat *it!* 1.11
s.t. is no* **bed *of roses* 9.10
put a **bee** *in s.o.'s bonnet* 4.4
tighten one's **belt** 1.25
make the **best** *of a bad bargain* 8.1
*kill two **birds** *with one stone* 6.4
*go full **blast** 1.21
breed/cause bad* **blood 5.2
burn (all) one's* **boats *(behind one)* 7.4
*make no **bones** *about s.t.* 7.12
rack one's* **brain(s) *(over s.t.)* 1.10
beat one's **brains** *out* 1.10
saw off the **branch** *one is sitting on* 8.17
***break** *it to s.o. gently* 3.3
beat one's* **breast 2.2
make a clean **breast** *of s.t.* 4.14
drop a **brick** 5.7
*run into a **brick** *wall* 8.3
burn (all) one's* **bridges *(behind one)* 7.4
be on the **brink** 9.13
tell everyone and his **brother** 7.9
*kick the **bucket** 2.9
*put a **bug** *in s.o.'s ear* 4.4
grab/take the* **bull *by the horns* 6.5, *6.19
*hit the **bull's** *eye* 6.18
beat around the **bush** 7.5
let **bygones** *be bygones* 9.6

C
*be in **cahoots** *with s.o.* 5.4
*that takes the **cake** 9.4
build a house of **cards** 1.13
lay/put one's **cards** *on the table* 4.22
*put the **cart** *before the horse* 8.9
***cash** *in on s.t.* 6.11
*build **castles** *in the air/Spain* 1.13
let the **cat** *out of the bag* 4.23
add/put in one's two* **cents *worth* 4.13
fall out of **character** 2.20
keep a **check** *on s.o.* 4.11
keep/hold s.o. in* **check 4.11
*pull the **chestnuts** *out of the fire (for s.o.)* *6.12, 6.24
keep one's **chin** *up* 1.17
*sail under false **colors** 2.6
show one's (true)* **colors 1.3
strike one's **colors** 2.6
come to **nothing** 9.1
have s.t. well under **control** 6.7
cost next to **nothing** 9.16
be (as) **cool** *as a* **cucumber** 1.14

D
not worth a (tinker's)* **damn 9.8
keep s.o. up to* **date 4.8
*it **dawns** *on s.o.* 1.12
carry the **day** 6.14
save (s.t.) for a rainy* **day 6.10
s.t. is **dead** *and buried* 9.6
*conjure up the **devil** 8.15
speak/talk of the **devil** 8.15
go to the **dogs** 2.13, 2.21
*go down the **drain** 9.1
be (securely) in the* **driver's *seat* 6.16
beat the **drum** *for s.o./s.t.* 6.13
bite the **dust** 2.9
*throw **dust** *in s.o.'s eyes* 3.4

E
talk s.o.'s* **ear *off* 2.12
put all one's* **eggs *in one basket* 7.17
*make both **ends** *meet* 6.3
*not bat an **eye(lash)** 1.14
give s.o. the **eye** 3.2
turn a blind **eye** *to* 4.1
*make **eyes** *at s.o.* 3.2

F
*put a brave **face** *on it* 1.15
talk oneself blue in the **face** 2.1
fall **through** 9.1
set the **fashion** 1.19
commit a **faux-pas** 5.7
***feel** *s.o. out* 4.19

get back on one's feet 1.24
help s.o. back on his/her feet 3.11
*sweep s.o. off his/her feet 3.7
play second fiddle to s.o. 4.5, 4.10
be spoiling for a fight 2.11
wrap s.o. around one's little finger 4.20
*slip through s.o.'s fingers 5.15
play with fire 7.18
*hoist/show/run up the white flag 8.14
fan the flames 8.8
not hurt a fly 3.6
have one's foot in the door 6.22
*put one's foot in it 5.7
*add fuel to the fire/flames 8.8
*not make a big fuss about s.t. 7.1

G
*see through s.o.'s (little) game 4.12
lead s.o. up the garden path 5.17
get tough with s.o. 1.20
give as good as one gets 5.18
*give it to s.o. straight (from the shoulder) 4.17
give s.o. tit for tat 5.18
*treat/handle s.o. with kid gloves 3.5
go it alone 2.14
*give s.o. the go-ahead 4.9
*be a godsend 9.5
*s.t. goes without saying 9.7
hear s.t. through the grapevine 3.3
grin and bear it 8.1
*have a firm grip on s.t. 6.7
be grist to s.o.'s mill 5.8
fall on fertile ground 9.18
*stand one's ground 6.9
*tread on delicate ground 7.7
*be on one's guard (against s.t.) 7.15
gun for s.o. 5.13
*bring all one's guns to bear on s.t./s.o. 6.6
bring up the big guns 6.6

H
*be/get in each other's hair 5.9
get in s.o.'s hair 5.9
*not harm/hurt a hair on s.o.'s head 3.6
split hairs (over s.t.) 8.18
give s.o. a hand 3.1
have s.t. on hand 6.7, 9.7
have s.t. well in hand 6.7
*lend s.o. a helping hand 3.1
*play (right) into s.o.'s hand 5.11
*fly off the handle 2.10
*wash one's hands of s.t. 7.10
have s.t. handy 6.7
hang in there 1.17
bury the hatchet 2.11

*bury/hide one's head in the sand 8.6
*have s.o.'s head 5.12
*ram/beat/knock one's head against a wall 8.5
talk one's head off 2.1
put/lay one's head together 4.7
pour one's heart out (to s.o.) 4.21
*move heaven and earth 6.8
*s.t. stinks to high heaven 9.9
*be hard on s.o.'s heels 4.2
dig one's heels in 6.9
follow on the heels of 4.2
stay on s.o.'s heels 4.2
take to one's heels 1.18
*take the helm 6.21
risk one's hide 1.9
*hightail it out of there 1.11
head for the hills 1.18
*give s.o. a broad hint 3.3, *4.18
*give s.o. a gentle hint *3.3, 4.18
*live high off the hog 1.5
get on one's high horse 2.15
*go into a huddle 4.7

I
break the ice 3.12
put s.t. on ice 7.6
*strike while the iron is hot *6.5, 6.19, 7.7
*not make a big issue of s.t. 7.1

K
keep s.o. posted 4.8
*pay s.o. back in kind 5.18

L
*see how the land lies 7.5
s.t. falls right into one's lap 6.17
live in the lap of luxury 1.5
rest on one's laurels 1.6
find out the lay of the land 7.5
turn over a new leaf 9.2
*be in league with s.o. 5.4
*let it pass 4.1
*let oneself in for s.t. 8.2
*not let s.o./s.t. get one down 4.15
live the life of Riley 1.5
*take one's life in one's hands 1.8
(finally) see the light 1.12
be the limit 9.4
*get out of line 2.14
toe the line 2.14
*dare (to) enter/venture into the lion's den 7.13
*keep a stiff upper lip 1.17
not trust the look of things 7.8

M

*make oneself scarce 1.18
*make s.o. shape up 4.16
*hit the mark 6.18
make one's mark 6.18
*make a mess of things 8.7
try s.o.'s mettle 4.19
make mincemeat out of s.o. 5.10
*throw a monkey wrench into the works 8.11
*happen (only) once in a blue moon 9.12
get a move on 6.15
*be music to s.o.'s ears 5.8
go and face the music 8.1
put a muzzle on s.o. 5.20

N

hit the nail on the head 6.18, 6.23
break one's (s.o.'s) neck 2.19, 5.19
*stick one's neck out 1.9
risk one's neck 1.9
*feather one's nest 8.12
look out for number One 8.12

O

*rest on one's oars 1.6
pour oil on troubled waters 8.8
give s.o. the once-over 4.19

P

mind one's P's and Q's 1.22
*howl with the pack 2.18
*bear/carry off the palm 6.14
cost a pretty penny 9.16
s.t.'s no picnic 9.10
that's a piece of cake 9.10
*swallow the bitter pill *8.1, 8.19
pin s.o. down 5.14
be a pipedream 1.13
s.t. is as plain as can be / day 9.7
*play it safe 1.16
*adorn oneself with borrowed plumes 2.5
line one's own pocket 8.12
go to pot 9.1
*s.t. sets a precedent 9.14
*beat/grind s.o. to a pulp 5.10
not pull one's punches 1.1
put it mildly 3.2

Q

pick a quarrel 2.11

R

*see through s.o.'s racket 4.12
vent one's rage (on s.o.) 2.10
break rank 2.14
*smell a rat 7.8
get a reading on s.o. 4.19
get a tighter rein on s.o. 6.21

give free rein to s.o. 4.6
*keep a tight rein on s.o. *4.6, 6.21
*take the reins 4.6, *6.21
*put up (a) fierce resistance (against s.t.) 7.11
take s.o. for a ride 5.6
ride roughshod over s.o. 3.5
*end up on the rocks 2.16
*bring things under one roof 7.14
*shout s.t. from the roof-tops *7.9, 9.15
*rule the roost 4.5
keep s.o. on the run 4.8

S

give s.o. the sack 5.12
never say die 4.15
*throw a scare into s.o. 5.3
appear on the scene 7.3
*put s.t. on the shelf *7.2, 7.6
the shoe is on the other foot 9.2
*call the shots 1.2
*put one's shoulder to the wheel 6.20
steal the show from s.o. 5.21
take s.o.'s side 3.10
*drop out of sight 7.3
*get/have s.t. handed to one on a silver platter 6.17
*it's six of one and half-a-dozen of the other 9.11
*be on the skids 2.13
*make it by the skin of one's teeth 1.7
save one's (own) skin 1.7, 1.26
reach for the sky 6.3
that's easy sledding 9.10
*have s.t. up one's sleeve 8.13
*laugh up one's sleeve 2.4
roll up one's sleeves 1.23
go up in smoke 9.1
*get s.t. for a song 6.2
make a song and dance about s.t. 7.1
sound s.o. out 4.19, 7.5
*put a spoke in s.o.'s wheel 5.1
*blow one's stack 2.8
*stand up for s.o. 3.10
*measure everything by the same standards 7.16
*see stars 2.3
step in it 5.7
*stick up for s.o. 3.10
leave no stone unturned 6.8
*put s.t. into cold storage 7.2, *7.6
pull strings 1.2, 1.11
live in grand style 1.5
follow suit 1.3
*give s.o. moral support 3.9

T
*keep (close) **tab(s)** on s.o.   4.3
*the **tables** are turned   9.2
 turn the **tables**   9.2
*(creep away) with one's **tail** between one's legs   8.10
*take s.o. **in**   *5.14, 5.16
*be **taken** in by s.o.   5.14, *5.16
***talk** oneself hoarse   2.1
*it's the **talk** of the town   9.15
 be right on **target**   6.18
*hit the **target**   6.18
 give s.o. a **taste** of his/her own medicine   5.18
 lose one's **temper**   2.10
 have everything under one's **thumb**   1.2
 twiddle one's **thumbs**   1.6
 the **tide** has turned   9.2
 swim with the **tide**   2.18
*not worth a **tinker's** damn   9.8
 hold/mind your **tongue**   1.22
 fight **tooth** and nail against s.t.   7.11
*blow one's **top**   2.8
*be **touch** and go   9.13
*throw in the **towel**   *2.7, 2.21
*paint the **town** (red)   6.13
 be off the beaten **track**   8.4
*be on the wrong **track**   8.4
 get on the **track** of s.t./s.o.   4.12
 make **tracks**   1.18
*lure s.o. into a **trap**   5.5, *5.6
*walk into s.o.'s **trap**   *5.5, 5.6
 bark up the wrong **tree**   8.4
 be up to s.o.'s **tricks**   4.12
 trip s.o. up   5.1
 play one's last **trump**   7.19
*change one's **tune**   1.20
 dance to another **tune**   4.10
*dance to s.o. else's **tune**   4.10
*call the **tune**   *1.19, 4.5

U
*that's the **upshot** of the matter   9.3
 be quick/slow on the **uptake**   1.12

W
*go on the **warpath**   2.11
 keep a (close/sharp) **watch** on s.o./s.t.   4.3
*that is **water** over the dam / under the bridge   9.6
*tell s.o. s.t. in a roundabout **way**   3.3
*drop/fall by the **wayside**   2.17
*spread like **wildfire**   9.17
 get **wind** of s.t.   7.20
*tilt at **windmills**   8.16
*take the **wheel**   6.21
*pull the **wool** over s.o.'s eyes   5.17
 take s.o. at his/her **word**   3.13
*not mince **words**   1.1
*weigh one's **words**   1.22

Y
*measure everything with the same **yardstick**   7.16

Z
zero in on s.t.   5.14

* * * * *

GERMAN INDEX

A
in den sauren **Apfel** beißen   8.1
jdm unter die **Arme** greifen   3.1
die **Ärmel** hochkrempeln   1.23
den **Ast** absägen, auf dem man sitzt   8.17
nicht viel **Aufheben(s)** von etwas machen   7.1
ein **Auge** zudrücken   4.1
jdm schöne **Augen** machen   3.2

B
etwas auf die lange **Bank** schieben   7.2
für etwas auf die **Barrikaden** gehen/steigen   6.1
jdm das/ein **Bein** stellen   5.1
jdm wieder auf die **Beine** helfen   3.11
(wieder) auf die **Beine** kommen   1.24
von der **Bildfläche** verschwinden   7.3
in die **Binsen** gehen   9.1

das **Blatt** hat sich gewendet   9.2
kein **Blatt** vor den Mund nehmen   1.1
etwas durch die **Blume** sagen   3.3
böses **Blut** erregen   5.2
jdn ins **Bockshorn** jagen   5.3
auf fruchtbaren **Boden** fallen   9.18
jdn zu **Brei** schlagen / siehe 5.10
alle **Brücken** hinter sich abbrechen   7.4
sich an die **Brust** schlagen   2.2
(bei jdm) auf den **Busch** klopfen   7.5
etwas für ein **Butterbrot** bekommen   6.2

D
mit jdm unter einer **Decke** stecken   5.4
sich nach der **Decke** strecken   6.3
jdm blauen **Dunst** vormachen   3.4

E
jdn behandeln wie ein rohes **Ei**   3.5
sich etwas **einbrocken**   8.2

das Eis brechen 3.12
etwas auf(s) Eis legen 7.6
ein heißes Eisen anfassen 7.7
das Ende vom Lied sein 9.3
die Engel im Himmel pfeifen/singen hören 2.3

F
alle Fäden in der Hand halten 1.2
jdm in die Falle gehen 5.5
jdn in die Falle locken 5.6
Farbe bekennen 1.3
das schlägt dem Faß den Boden aus 9.4
etwas auf eigene Faust tun 1.4
sich ins Fäustchen lachen 2.4
sich mit fremden Federn schmücken 2.5
jdm das Fell über die Ohren ziehen / siehe 5.17
jdm auf den Fersen folgen 4.2
ins Fettnäpfchen treten 5.7
mit dem Feuer spielen 7.18
jdm auf die Finger sehen/schauen 4.3
jdn um den kleinen Finger wickeln 4.20
unter falscher Flagge segeln 2.6
jdm Flausen in den Kopf setzen / siehe 4.4
zwei Fliegen mit einer Klappe schlagen 6.4
die Flinte ins Korn werfen 2.7
jdm einen Floh ins Ohr setzen 4.4
für jdn ein gefundenes Fressen sein 5.8
dem Frieden nicht trauen 7.8
auf großem Fuß leben 1.5
den Fuß in der Tür haben 6.22

G
etwas in Gang setzen/bringen / siehe 6.15
das ist gehüpft wie gesprungen / siehe 9.11
die erste Geige spielen 4.5
nach jds Geige tanzen 4.10
die Gelegenheit beim Schopf packen 6.5
ein Geschenk des Himmels sein 9.5
ein grobes/schweres Geschütz auffahren 6.6
jdm etwas in Gesicht sagen / siehe 1.1
Gift und Galle spucken 2.8
Gleiches mit Gleichem vergelten / siehe 5.18
etwas an die große Glocke hängen 7.9
auf Granit beißen 8.3
ins Gras beißen 2.9
über etwas ist längst Gras gewachsen 9.6
den Gürtel enger schnallen 1.25

H
jdm kein Haar krümmen 3.6
Haare spalten 8.18
sich in den Haaren liegen 5.9
aus jdm Hackfleisch machen 5.10
sich/jdm den Hals brechen 2.19, 5.19
etwas fest in der Hand haben 6.7
etwas liegt (klar) auf der Hand 9.7

die Hände in den Schoß legen 1.6
seine Hände in Unschuld waschen 7.10
sich mit Händen und Füßen gegen etwas wehren 7.11
das Handtuch werfen 2.21
mit heiler Haut davonkommen 1.7
aus der Haut fahren 2.10
seine Haut zu Markte tragen 1.8
seine Haut retten 1.26
alle Hebel in Bewegung setzen 6.8
kein Hehl aus etwas machen 7.12
keinen roten Heller wert sein 9.8
(jdm) sein Herz ausschütten 4.21
aus seinem Herzen keine Mördergrube machen / siehe 7.12
zum Himmel stinken/schreien 9.9
sich auf die Hinterbeine stellen 6.9
sich in die Höhle des Löwen begeben/wagen 7.13
auf dem Holzweg sein 8.4
das ist kein Honiglecken 9.10
etwas unter einen Hut bringen 7.14
(vor etwas) auf der Hut sein 7.15

J
das ist Jacke wie Hose 9.11
nur alle Jubeljahre einmal vorkommen 9.12

K
etwas über einen Kamm scheren 7.16
jdn an der Kandare halten 4.6
etwas auf die hohe Kante legen 6.10
aus etwas Kapital schlagen 6.11
die Karre aus dem Dreck ziehen 6.12
alles auf eine Karte setzen 7.17
jdm eine Karte in die Hand spielen 5.11
die Karten (offen) auf den Tisch legen 4.22
die Kastanien aus dem Feuer holen 6.24
die Katze aus dem Sack lassen 4.23
auf der Kippe stehen 9.13
Kopf und Kragen riskieren 1.9
jds Kopf rollen lassen 5.12
den Kopf in den Sand stecken 8.6
jdm den Kopf verdrehen 3.7
mit dem Kopf durch die Wand wollen 8.5
sich den Kopf zerbrechen 1.10
die Köpfe zusammenstecken 4.7
jdn aufs Korn nehmen 5.13
jdm platzt der Kragen / siehe 2.10
jdn aufs Kreuz legen 5.14
das Kriegsbeil ausgraben 2.11

L
für jdn eine Lanze brechen 3.8
jdm durch die Lappen gehen 5.15
jdn auf dem Laufenden halten 4.8

sich wie ein **Lauffeuer** *verbreiten* / siehe 9.17
jdm auf den **Leim** *gehen* 5.16
Leine *ziehen* 1.11
jdm geht ein **Licht** *auf* 1.12
jdm grünes **Licht** *geben* 4.9
jdn hinters **Licht** *führen* 5.17
jdm ein **Loch** *in den Bauch reden* 2.12
in die **Luft** *gehen* / siehe 2.10
Luftschlösser *bauen* 1.13

M
jdm einen **Maulkorb** *umhängen* 5.20
gute **Miene** *zum bösen Spiel machen* 1.15
keine **Miene** *verziehen* 1.14
Mist *bauen* 8.7
sich den **Mund** *in Fransen reden* 2.1
jdm mit gleicher **Münze** *heimzahlen* 5.18

N
den **Nagel** *auf den Kopf treffen* 6.23
jdm ins **Netz** *gehen* 5.5
auf **Nummer** *sicher gehen* 1.16

O
Öl *ins Feuer gießen* 8.8
die **Ohren** *steif halten* 1.17

P
auf die **Pauke** *hauen* 6.13
nach jds **Pfeife** *tanzen* 4.10
das **Pferd** *beim Schwanz aufzäumen* 8.9
die bittere **Pille** *schlucken* 8.19
wie ein begossener **Pudel** *(davonschleichen)* 8.10

R
unter die **Räder** *kommen* 2.13
aus der **Reihe** *tanzen* 2.14
das **Rennen** *machen* 6.14
aus der **Rolle** *fallen* 2.20
etwas ins **Rollen** *bringen* 6.15
auf dem hohen **Roß** *sitzen* 2.15
jdm den **Rücken** *stärken* 3.9
das **Ruder** *in die Hand nehmen* 6.21

S
andere **Saiten** *aufziehen* / siehe 1.20
Sand *ins Getriebe streuen* 8.11
(fest/sicher) im **Sattel** *sitzen* 6.16
jdn in **Schach** *halten* 4.11
sein **Schäfchen** *ins Trockene bringen* 8.12

jdm die **Schau** *stehlen* 5.21
Schiffbruch *erleiden* 2.16
etwas im **Schilde** *führen* 8.13
jdm auf die **Schliche** *kommen* 4.12
jdm fällt etwas in den **Schoß** 6.17
etwas macht **Schule** 9.14
keinen **Schuß** *Pulver wert sein* / siehe 9.8
ins **Schwarze** *treffen* 6.18
die **Segel** *streichen* 8.14
seinen **Senf** *dazugeben* 4.13
die **Spatzen** *pfeifen es von den Dächern* 9.1
jdm die **Stange** *halten* 3.10
sich aus dem **Staube** *machen* 1.18
den **Stein** *ins Rollen bringen* / siehe 6.15
den **Stier** *bei den Hörnern packen* 6.19
auf der **Strecke** *bleiben* 2.17

T
den **Teufel** *an die Wand malen* 8.15
reinen **Tisch** *machen* 4.14
den **Ton** *angeben* 1.19
eine andere **Tonart** *anschlagen* 1.20
auf vollen **Touren** *laufen* 1.21
den letzten **Trumpf** *ausspielen* 7.19

U
sich nicht **unterkriegen** *lassen* 4.15

V
Vogel-Strauß *Politik treiben* / siehe 8.6
jdn auf **Vordermann** *bringen* 4.16

W
die **Waffen** *strecken* / siehe 8.14
jdm reinen **Wein** *einschenken* 4.17
etwas wird die **Welt** *nicht kosten* 9.16
von etwas **Wind** *bekommen* 7.20
nicht viel **Wind** *um etwas machen* / siehe 7.1
sich mit **Windeseile** *verbreiten* 9.17
gegen **Windmühlen** *kämpfen* 8.16
jdm einen **Wink** *mit dem Zaunpfahl geben* 4.18
mit den **Wölfen** *heulen* 2.18
jdn beim **Wort** *nehmen* 3.13

Z
jdm auf den **Zahn** *fühlen* 4.19
sich tüchtig ins **Zeug** *legen* 6.20
die **Zügel** *in die Hand nehmen* 6.21
die **Zunge** *im Zaum halten* 1.22